Mysteries of the Great Operas

By Max Heindel

*FAUST, PARSIFAL, THE RING OF THE
NIEBELUNG, TANNHAUSER, LOHENGRIN*

FIFTH EDITION

The Rosicrucian Fellowship
International Headquarters
Mt. Ecclesia
Oceanside, California, U.S.A.

ENGLAND:
L. N. Fowler & Co., Ltd., 29 Ludgate Hill
London, E. C. 4

Copyright, 1921
by
MRS. MAX HEINDEL

FIRST PRINTING OF
PAPER COVER EDITION
JUNE 1975

FELLOWSHIP PRESS
OCEANSIDE, CALIF.

Table of Contents

                                                                                              Page

FAUST

Chapter I.
        Divine Discord 5

Chapter II.
        The Sorrows of the Seeking Soul 12

Chapter III.
        The Sorrows of the Seeking Soul (cont.) 19

Chapter IV.
        Selling His Soul to Satan 26

Chapter V.
        Selling His Soul to Satan (cont.) 33

Chapter VI.
        The Wages of Sin and the Ways of Salvation 40

PARSIFAL

Chapter VII.
        Wagner's Mystic Music Drama 49

THE RING OF THE NIEBELUNG

Chapter VIII.
        The Rhine Maidens 71

Chapter IX.
        The Ring of the Gods 78

Chapter X.
        The Valkuerie 85

Table of Contents, Continued

Page

Chapter XI.
    Siegfried, the Truth Seeker 93
Chapter XII.
    The Battle of Truth and Error 101
Chapter XIII.
    Rebirth and the Lethal Drink 109
Chapter XIV.
    The Twilight of the Gods 117

TANNHAUSER

Chapter XV.
    The Pendulum of Joy and Sorrow 127
Chapter XVI.
    Minstrels, the Initiates of the Middle Ages 135
Chapter XVII.
    The Unpardonable Sin 142
Chapter XVIII.
    The Rod that Budded 149

LOHENGRIN

Chapter XIX.
    The Knight of the Swan 157
    Index 167

Faust

Divine Discord

Faust

Chapter I

DIVINE DISCORD

WHEN the name Faust is mentioned, the majority of educated people at once think of Gounod's presentations upon the stage. Some admire the music, but the story itself does not seem to particularly impress them. As it appears there, it seems to be the unfortunately all too common story of a sensualist who betrays a young unsuspecting girl and then leaves her to expiate her folly and suffer for her trustfulness. The touch of magic and witchery which enters into the play is thought of by most people as only the fancies of an author who has used them to make the sordid, everyday conditions more interesting.

When Faust is taken by Mephistopheles to the underworld and Marguerite is borne to heaven upon angelic wings at the conclusion of the play, it appears to them to be just the ordinary moral to give the story a goody-goody ending.

A small minority know that Gounod's opera is based upon the drama written by Goethe. And those who have studied the two parts of his presentation of Faust, gain a very different idea from that presented by the play. Only the few who are illuminated mystics, see in the play written by Goethe the unmistakable hand of an enlightened fellow Initiate, and realize fully the great cosmic significance contained therein.

Be it very clearly understood that the story of Faust is a myth as old as mankind. Goethe presented it clad in a proper mystic light, illuminating one of the greatest problems of the day, the relation and struggle between Freemasonry and Catholicism, which we have considered from another viewpoint in a former book.

We have often said in our literature, that a myth is a veiled symbol containing a great cosmic truth, a conception which differs radically from the generally accepted one. As we give picture books to our children to convey lessons beyond their intellectual grasp, so the great Teachers gave infant humanity these pictorial symbols, and thus, unconsciously to mankind, an appreciation of the ideals presented has been etched into our finer vehicles.

As a seed germinates unseen in the ground ere it can flower above the visible surface of the Earth, so these etchings traced by the myths upon our finer, invisible vestures have put us into a state of receptivity where we readily take to higher ideals and rise above the sordid conditions of the material world. These ideals would have been submerged by the lower nature, had it not been prepared for ages by the agency of just such myths as Faust, Parsifal, and kindred tales.

Like the story of Job the scene of the Faust myth has its beginning in heaven at a convocation of the Sons of Seth, Lucifer among them. The ending is also in heaven as presented by Goethe. As it is very different from that which is commonly presented upon the stage, we stand face to face with a gigantic problem. In fact, the Faust myth depicts the evolution of mankind during the present epoch. It also shows us how the Sons of Seth and the Sons of Cain each play their part in the work of the world.

It has always been the custom of the writer to stick as closely to his subject as possible, so that any phase of the philosophy under consideration might receive the full force of concentrated illumination so far as was possible to give it. But sometimes circumstances justify departure from the main trend of the argument, and our consideration of the Faust myth is one of them. Were we to discourse upon this subject only in so far as it has a bearing upon the problem of Freemasonry and Catholicism, we should have to return to the subject later, in order to illuminate other points of vital interest in the unfoldment of soul as the work of the human race. We therefore trust that digressions may not be criticized.

In the opening scene, three of the Sons of God, Planetary Spirits, are represented as bowing before the Grand Architect of the Universe, singing songs of the spheres in their adoration of the Ineffable Being who is the source of life, the author of all manifestation. Goethe represents one of these supernal Spirits of the stars as saying:

> "The sun intones its ancient song,
> 'Mid rival chant of brother spheres,
> Its predestined course it speeds along,
> In thund'rous march throughout the years."

Modern scientific instruments have been invented, whereby in laboratory tests light waves are transmuted to sound, thus demonstrating in the Physical World the mystic maxim of the identity of these manifestations. That which was patent formerly only to the mystic who was able to raise his consciousness to the Region of Concrete Thought, is now also sensed by the scientist. The song of the spheres, first publicly mentioned by Pythagoras, is not therefore, to be regarded as an empty idea originated in the too vivid imagination of poetical minds nor as the hallucination of a demented brain.

Goethe meant every word he said. The stars have each their own keynote, and they travel about the Sun at such varying rates of speed, that their position now cannot be duplicated until twenty-seven thousand years have passed. Thus the harmony of the heavens changes at every moment of life, and as it changes, so does the world alter its ideas and ideals. The circle dance of the marching orbs to the tune of the celestial symphony created by them marks man's progress along the path we call evolution.

But it is a mistaken idea to think that constant harmony is pleasing. Music thus expressed would become monotonous; we should weary of the continued harmony. In fact, music would lose its charm were not dissonance interspersed at frequent intervals. The closer a composer can come to discord without actually entering it in the score, the more pleasing will be his composition when given life through musical instruments. Similarly in the song of the spheres, we could never reach individuality and the selfhood towards which all evolution trends, without the divine discord.

Therefore, the Book of Job designates Satan as being one of the Sons of God. And the Faust myth speaks of Lucifer as also present in the convocation, which takes place during the opening chapter of the story. From him comes the saving note of dissonance which forms a contrast to the celestial harmony; and as the brightest light throws the deepest shadow, Lucifer's voice enhances the beauty of the celestial song.

While the other Planetary Spirits bow down in adoration when they contemplate the works of the Master Architect as revealed in the universe, Lucifer sounds the note of criticism, of blame, in the following words directed against the masterpiece of God, the king of creatures, man:

> "Of suns and worlds I nothing have to say,
> I see alone man's self-inflicted pains;
> That little world god still his stamp retains,
> As wondrous now as on the primal day.
> Better he might have fared, poor wight,
> Had You withheld the heavenly light;
> Reason he names it, but doth use it so,
> That he more brutish than brutes doth grow."

This from the viewpoint of former generations may sound sacrilegious, but in the greater light of modern times we can understand that even in so exalted a being as that designated by the name of God, there must be growth. We can sense the striving after still greater abilities, the contemplation of future universes offering improved facilities for those evolutions of other Virgin Spirits, which are a result of the imperfections noted in the scheme of manifestation by its exalted Author. Furthermore, as "in Him we live and move and have our being," so the discordant note sounded by the Lucifer Spirits would also rise within Him. It would not be an outside agency which called attention to mistakes or took Him to task, but His own divine recognition of an imperfection to be transmuted into greater good.

In the Bible we read that Job was a perfect man, and in the Faust myth the bearer of the title role is designated a servant of God, for naturally the problem of unfoldment, of greater growth, must be solved by the most highly advanced. Ordinary individuals, or those who are lower in the scale of evolution, have still that part of the road to travel which has already been covered by such as Faust and Job, who are the vanguard of the race, and who are looked upon by ordinary humanity in the same way that Lucifer describes them, namely as fools and freaks:

"Poor fool, his food and drink are not of earth,
An inward impulse hurries him afar;
Himself, half conscious of his frenzied mood;
From heaven claimeth he the fairest star,
And from the earth he craves the highest, best;
And all that's near and all that's far,
Can never still the cravings of his breast."

For such people a new and higher path must be opened to give them greater opportunities for growth; hence the answer of God:

"Though in perplexity he serves me now,
I soon will lead him where the light appears;
When buds the sapling doth the gardener know,
That flow'r and fruit shall grace its coming years."

Chapter II

THE SORROWS OF THE SEEKING SOUL

AS EXERCISE is necessary to the development of physical muscle, so development of the moral nature is accomplished through temptation. The Ego being given choice, may exercise it in whatever direction it chooses, for it learns just as well by its mistakes as by right action in the first place, perhaps even better. Therefore, in the Job myth, the devil is permitted to tempt; and in the Faust myth he makes the request:

"My Lord, if I may lead him as I choose,
 I wager Thou him yet wilt lose."
To this the Lord replies:

" 'Tis granted thee! Divert
This spirit from its primal source,
Him mayst thou seize, thy power exert,
If he will go the downward course.
But stand ashamed when thou art forced to own,
A good man in his darkest aberration
Still knows the path that leadeth to salvation.
Go, thou art free to act without control.
I do not cherish hate for such as thee;

Of all the spirits of negation
The cynic is least wearisome to Me.
Man is too prone, activity to shirk,
And undisturbed in rest he fain would live;
Hence this companion purposely I give
Who stirs, excites, and must as devil work.
But ye, O faithful Sons of God, none wronging,
Rejoice in all of everliving beauty,
The everliving, evergrowing, and becoming;
Now gird yourselves about with love and duty.''

Thus the plot is ready and Faust is about to become enmeshed in the snares which beset the path of every seeking soul. The following lines show the beneficent purpose and the necessity of temptation. The Spirit is an integral part of God; primarily *innocent*, but not virtuous. Virtue is a positive quality developed by taking a firm stand for the right in temptation, or by the suffering endured in consequence of wrongdoing. Thus the prologue in heaven gives to the Faust myth its highest value as a guide, and its encouragement to the seeking soul. It shows the eternal purpose behind the earthly conditions which cause pain and sorrow.

Goethe next introduces us to Faust himself, who is standing in his darkened study. He is engaged in introspection and retrospection:

"I have, alas! philosophy, medicine, and law,
Theology I too have studied, pshaw!

Now here I stand with all my lore,
A fool no wiser than before.
I thought to better humankind,
To elevate the human mind;
I have not worked for goods nor treasure,
Nor worldly honor, rank, nor pleasure.
With books I all my life have striven,
But now to magic I am given;
And hope through spirit voice and might,
Secrets veiled to bring to light.
That I no more with aching brow,
Need speak of what I nothing know.
Woe's me! Still prisoned in the gloom
Of this abhorred and musty room,
Where heaven's dear light itself doth pass
But dimly through the painted glass.
Up! forth into the distant land.
Is not this book of mystery
By Nostradamus' magic hand,
An all sufficient guide? Thou'lt see
The courses of the stars unrolled,
When Nature doth her thoughts unfold
To thee. Thy soul shall rise and seek
Communion high with her to hold.''

A lifetime of study has brought Faust no real knowledge. The conventional sources of learning prove barren in the end. The scientist may think God a superfluity; he may believe that life consists in chemical action and reaction—that is, when he starts. But the deeper he delves into matter, the greater the mysteries that beset his path, and at last he will be forced to abandon further research or believe in God as a Spirit whose life invests every atom of matter. Faust has come to that point. He says that he has not worked for gold "nor treasure, nor worldly honor, rank, nor pleasure." He has striven from love of research and has come to the point where he sees that a spirit world is about us all; and through this world, through magic, he now aspires to a higher, more real knowledge than that contained in books.

A tome, written by the famous Nostradamus is in his hand, and on opening it he beholds the sign of the macrocosm. The power contained therein opens to his consciousness a part of the world he is seeking, and in an ecstasy of joy he exclaims:

"Ah! at this spectacle through every sense,
What sudden ecstasy of joy is flowing;
I feel new rapture, hallowed and intense.
Now of the wise man's words I learn the sense:
Unlocked the spirit world is lying,
Thy senses shut, thy heart is dead;
Up, scholar! lave with zeal undying
Thine earthly breast in morning red.
How all that lives and works is ever blending,
Weaves one vast whole from Being's ample range,
See powers celestial rising and descending,

Their golden buckets' ceaseless interchange.
Their flight on rapture breathing pinions winging,
From heaven to earth the rhythm bringing.''

But again the pendulum swings back. As an attempt to gaze directly into the brilliant light of the Sun would result in shattering the retina of the eye, so the audacious attempt to fathom the Infinite results in failure and the seeking soul is thrown from the ecstasy of joy into the darkness of despair:

"A wondrous show, but ah! a show alone.
Where shall I grasp thee, infinite nature, where?
Ye breasts, ye fountains of all life whereon
Hang heaven and earth, from which the withered
      heart
For solace yearns. Ye still impart
Your sweet and fostering tides; where are ye—
      where?
Ye gush, and I must languish in despair.''

We must first understand the lower before we can successfully aspire to a higher knowledge. To rant and rave of worlds beyond, of finer bodies, when we have little conception of the vehicles with which we work every day and the environment in which we move, is the height of folly. "Man, know thyself" is a sound teaching. The only safety lies in climbing the ladder rung by rung, never attempting a new step until we have made ourselves secure, until we are poised and balanced upon the one where we stand. Many a soul can echo from its own experience the despair embodied in the words of Faust.

Foolishly he has started at the highest point. He has suffered disappointment, but does not yet understand that he must begin at the bottom; so he commences an evocation of the Earth Spirit:

> "Earth Spirit, Thou to me art nigher,
> E'en now my strength is rising higher,
> Courage I feel, abroad the world to dare,
> The woe of earth, the bliss of earth, to bear;
> With storms to wrestle, brave the lightning glare,
> And 'mid the crashing shipwreck not despair.
> Clouds gather o'er me, obscure the moon's light,
> The lamp's flame is quenched with darkness of night.
> Vapors are rising, flashing and red,
> Beams of them dartingly, piercing my head;
> I am seized with a sickening, shuddering dread.
> Spirit, prayer-compelled, 'tis Thou
> Art hovering near, unveil Thyself now.
> My heart I gladly surrender to Thee;
> Thou must appear, if life be free."

As we have said in *The Rosicrucian Cosmo-Conception,* and as we have further elucidated in the Rosicrucian philosophy relative to a question concerning the Latin ritual in the Catholic Church, a name is a sound. Properly uttered, no matter by whom, it has a compelling influence over the intelligence it represents, and the word given in each degree of Initiation gives man access to a particular sphere of vibration, peopled by certain classes of Spirits. Therefore, as a tuning fork responds to a note of even pitch, so when Faust sounds *the name* of the Earth Spirit, it opens his consciousness to that all pervading presence.

And be it remembered that Faust's experience is not an isolated instance of what may happen under abnormal conditions. He is a symbol of the seeking soul. You and I are Fausts in a certain sense, for at some stage in our evolution we shall meet the Earth Spirit and realize the power of His name, properly uttered.

Chapter III

THE SORROWS OF THE SEEKING SOUL *(Continued)*

IN *The Star of Bethlehem, a Mystic Fact*, we endeavored to give students a glimpse of a certain phase of Initiation. Most of us walk about upon Earth and see only a seemingly dead mass, but one of the first facts revealed in our consciousness by Initiation is the living reality of the Earth Spirit. As the surface of our body is dead compared to the organs within, so the outer envelope of the Earth, being encrusted, gives no idea of the wonderful activity within. Upon the path of Initiation nine different layers are revealed, and in the center of this rolling sphere we meet the Spirit of the Earth face to face. It is actually true that it is "groaning and travailing" in the Earth for the sake of all, working and anxiously waiting for our manifestation as Sons of God so that, as the seeking soul which aspires to liberation is released from its dense body, the Earth Spirit also may be liberated from its body of death in which it is now confined for us.

The words of the Earth Spirit to Faust, as given by Goethe, offer splendid material for meditation, for they represent mystically what the candidate feels when he first realizes the actual reality of the Earth Spirit as a living presence, ever actively laboring for our uplift.

> "In the currents of life, in the action of storm
> I float and wave with billowy motion;
> Birth and the grave, a limitless ocean;
> A constant weaving, with change still rife,
> A restless heaving, a glowing life,
> Time's whizzing loom I've unceasingly trod;
> Thus weave I the living garment of God."

Of course, the Earth Spirit is not to be thought of as a larger man, or as having physical form other than the Earth itself. The vital body of Jesus, in which the Christ Spirit was focused prior to its actual ingress into the Earth, has the ordinary human form; it is preserved and is shown to the candidate at a certain point in his progression. Some day in the far future it will again house the benevolent Christ Spirit upon His return from the center of the Earth, when we shall have become etheric, and when He is ready to ascend to higher spheres, leaving us to be taught of the Father, whose religion will be higher than the Christian religion.

The Sorrows of the Seeking Soul

The esoteric truth that *when a Spirit enters by a certain door, it must also return the same way,* is taught by Goethe in connection with the initial appearance of Mephistopheles to Faust. Faust is not upon the regular path of Initiation. He has not earned admission nor the help of the Elder Brothers; he is seeking at the wrong door because of his impatience. Therefore he is spurned by the Earth Spirit and when having seemingly attained, is plunged from the pinnacle of joy to the pit of despair where he realizes that he has in reality failed.

> "I, God's own image, from this toil of clay
> Already free, who hailed
> The mirror of eternal truth unveiled,
> 'Mid light effulgent and celestial day,
> I, whose unfettered soul
> With penetrative glance aspired to flow
> Through nature's veins, and still creating know
> The life of gods . . . how am I punished now,
> One thunder word has hurled me from the goal!
> Spirit, I dare not lift me to thy sphere;
> What though my power compelled thee to appear,
> My art was futile to detain thee here.
> Fiercely didst thrust me from the realm of thought,
> Back on humanity's uncertain fate!
> Who'll teach me now? What ought I to forego?"

He thinks the sources of information are exhausted and that he may never attain to the real knowledge. And fearing the dull monotony of a plodding, ordinary existence, he grasps a phial of poison and is about to drink, when songs without, proclaim the risen Christ for it is Easter morning. At the thought, new hope stirs his soul. He is also further disturbed in his purpose by the knocking of Wagner, his friend.

Walking with the latter, Faust voices the cry of agony wrung from every aspiring soul in the awful struggle between the higher and lower natures. So long as we live worldly lives without higher aspirations, there is peace in our breasts. But once we have sensed the call of the Spirit, our equipoise is gone, and the more ardently we pursue the quest of the Grail, the fiercer is this inner struggle. Paul thought of himself as a wretched man because lower desires in the flesh combated the higher spiritual aspirations. Faust's words are of similar import:

"Two souls, alas, are housed within my breast,
And struggle there for undivided reign;
One to the earth with passionate desire
And closely clinging organs still adheres,
Above the mists the other does aspire
With sacred ardor unto purer spheres."

But he does not realize that there is no royal road to attainment, that each one must walk the path to peace alone. He thinks that Spirits can give him soul power ready for use:

"Oh, are there spirits in the air,
Who float 'twixt heaven and earth dominion wielding?
Stoop hither from your golden atmosphere;
Lead me to scenes, new life and fuller yielding.
A magic mantle did I but possess,
Abroad to waft me as on viewless wings,
I'd prize it far beyond most costly dress,
Nor change it for the robe of kings."

Because of this looking to others he is doomed to disappointment. "If thou art Christ help thyself," is the universal rule, and self-reliance is the cardinal virtue which aspirants are required to cultivate in the Western Mystery School. No one is allowed to lean on *Masters,* nor to blindly follow *Leaders.* The Brothers of the Rose Cross aim to emancipate the souls that come to them; to educate, to strengthen, and to make them *coworkers.* Philanthropists do not grow on every bush, and whoever looks to a Teacher to do more than point the way, will meet disappointment. No matter what their claims, no matter whether they come in the flesh, or as Spirits, no matter how spiritual they seem, Teachers positively cannot do for us the good deeds requisite to soul growth, assimilate them, nor give us the resulting soul power ready to use, any more than they can impart to us physical strength by eating our food. True, Faust the seeking soul, attracts a Spirit ready to serve him, but it is a Spirit of an undesirable nature, Lucifer. When Faust asks his name, he replies:

"The Spirit of Negation; the power that still
Works for good though scheming ill."

People or Spirits who offer to gratify our desires usually have an end in view.

Now we come to a point involving an important cosmic law which underlies various spiritualistic phenomena and also supports the unique teaching of The Rosicrucian Fellowship (and the Bible), that Christ will not return in a dense body but in a vital body. It also shows why He *must* return. Students will therefore do well to read very carefully:

Attracted by the mental attitude of Faust, Lucifer follows him into his study. On the floor just inside the door is a five pointed star with the two horns nearest the door. In the ordinary process of Nature the human Spirit enters its dense body during antenatal life and withdraws at death by way of the head. Invisible Helpers who have learned to transmute their sex force to soul power in the pituitary body, also leave and enter the dense body by way of the head; therefore, the pentagram *with one point upward,* symbolizes the aspiring soul who works in harmony with Nature.

The black magician, who has neither soul nor soul

power, also uses the sex force. He leaves and enters his body by way of the feet, the silver cord protruding from the sex organ. Therefore, the pentagram with two points upward is the symbol of black magic. Lucifer had no trouble in entering Faust's study, but when he wishes to leave after speaking with Faust, the single point bars his way. He requests Faust to remove the sign and the latter queries:

Faust: The pentagram your peace does mar,
       To me you, son of hell, make clear,
       How entered you, if this your exit bar?
       Where is the snare,
       Why through the window not withdraw?

Lucifer: For ghosts, devils, 'tis a law,
       Where we stole in, there we must forth;
         we're free
       The first to choose, but to the second, slaves
         are we.

Before A. D. 33 Jehovah guided our planet in its orbit and mankind on the path of evolution *from without*. On Golgotha, Christ entered the Earth which He now guides from within, and will until a sufficient number of our humanity have evolved the soul power necessary to float the Earth and guide our younger brothers. This requires ability to live in vital bodies, capable of levitation. The vital body of Jesus through which Christ entered the Earth is His only avenue of return to the Sun. Hence the Second Advent will be in Jesus' vital body.

Chapter IV

SELLING HIS SOUL TO SATAN

THE FAUST myth presents a curious situation in the meeting of the hero, who is the seeking soul, with different classes of Spirits. The Spirit of Faust, inherently good, feels drawn to the higher orders; it feels akin to the benevolent Earth Spirit, and bemoans the inability to detain it and learn from it. Face to face with the spirit of negation, who is only too willing to teach and to serve, he finds himself master in a certain sense, because that spirit cannot leave, over the symbol of the five pointed star in the position it is placed upon the floor. But both his inability to detain the Earth Spirit and obtain tuition from that exalted Being, and his mastery over the spirit of negation, are due to the fact that he has come into contact with them *by chance* and not by soul power evolved from within.

When Parsifal, the hero of another of these great soul myths, first visited the Castle of the Grail, he was asked how he had come there, and he answered "I know not." He just *happened* to enter the holy

Selling His Soul to Satan

place as a soul sometimes gets a glimpse of the celestial realms in a vision; but he could not stay in Mount Salvat. He was forced to go out into the world again and learn his lessons. Many years later he returned to the Castle of the Grail, weary and worn with the quest, and the same query again was asked: "How did you come here?" But this time his answer was different, for he said, "Through search and suffering I came."

That is the cardinal point which marks the great difference between persons who happen to come in contact with Spirits from superphysical realms by chance or stumble upon the solution of a law of Nature, and those, who by diligent research and particularly by *living the life*, attain to conscious Initiation into the secrets of Nature. The former do not know how to use this power intelligently and are therefore helpless. The latter are always masters of the forces they wield, while the others are the sport of anyone who wishes to take advantage of them.

Faust is the symbol of man, and humanity was first led by the Lucifer Spirits and the Angels of Jehovah. We are now looking to the Christ Spirit within the Earth as the Saviour to emancipate us from their selfish and negative influence.

Paul gives us a glimpse of the further evolution designed for us, when he says, that after Christ has established the kingdom, He will turn it over to the Father, who will then be all in all.

Faust, however, first seeks communication with the macrocosm, who is the Father. Like the heavenly centaur, Sagittarius, he aims his bow at the highest stars. He is not satisfied to begin at the bottom and work his way up gradually. When spurned by that sublime Being, he comes down one step in the scale and seeks communion with the Earth Spirit who also scorns him, for he cannot become the pupil of the good forces until he has conformed to their rules, so that he may enter the path of Initiation by the true door. Therefore, when he finds that the pentagram at the door holds the evil Spirit, he sees a chance to drive a bargain. He is ready to sell his soul to Satan.

As said before, however, he is too ignorant to successfully retain the mastery, and spirit power quickly clears away the obstructions and leaves Lucifer free. But though he departs from the chamber of Faust, he soon returns ready to barter for the seeking soul. He paints before Faust's eyes glowing pictures of how he may live his life over, how he may gratify his passions and desires. Faust, knowing that Lucifer is not disinterested, inquires what compensation he requires. To this, Lucifer answers:

"I pledge myself to be thy servant here,
At every beck and call alert to be;
But when we meet in yonder sphere,
Then shalt thou do the same for me."

Faust himself, adds a seemingly singular condition, regarding the time when the service of Lucifer shall terminate and his own earth life come to an end.

Strange as it seems, we have in the agreement of Lucifer and the clause proposed by Faust basic laws of evolution. By the Law of Attraction we are drawn into contact with kindred Spirits both here and hereafter. If we serve the good forces here and labor to lift ourselves, we find similarly minded company in this world and in the next, but if we love darkness rather than light, we find ourselves associated with the underworld here and hereafter also. There is no escape from this.

Furthermore, we are all "temple builders" working under the direction of God and His ministers, the divine Hierarchies. If we shirk the task set us in life, we are placed under conditions which will force us to learn. There is no rest nor peace upon the path of evolution and if we seek pleasure and joy to the exclusion of the work of life, the death knell soon comes. If ever we come to a point where we are ready to bid the passing hour stay, where we are so contented with conditions that we cease our efforts to progress, our existence is quickly terminated. It is a matter of observation, that people who retire from business to live only for the enjoyment of that which they have accumulated, soon pass out; while the man who changes his vocation for an avocation generally lives longer. Nothing is so apt to end an existence as inactivity. Therefore, as has been said, the laws of Nature are enunciated in the bargain of Lucifer and the condition added by Faust:

> "If e'er I be content in sloth or leisure,
> Then be that hour the last I see.
> When thou with flattery canst cajole me
> Till self-complaisant I shall be;
> When thou with pleasure canst befool me,
> Be that the final day for me.
> Whenever to the passing hour
> I say, 'Oh stay, thou art so fair!'
> Then unto thee I give the power
> To drag me down to deep despair.
> Then let my knell no longer linger,
> Then from my service thou art free;
> Fall from the clock the index finger,
> Be time all over then for me."

Lucifer requests Faust to sign with a *drop of blood*. And when asked the reason, he says cunningly, "Blood is a most peculiar essence." The Bible says it is the seat of the soul.

When the Earth was in process of condensation the invisible aura surrounding Mars, Mercury and Venus penetrated the Earth and the Spirits of these planets were in peculiar and close relation with humanity. Iron is a Mars metal, and by the admixture of iron

SELLING HIS SOUL TO SATAN

with the blood, oxidation is made possible; thus the inner heat required for the manifestation of an indwelling Spirit was obtained through the agency of the Lucifer Spirits from Mars. They are therefore responsible for the conditions under which the Ego is immured in the physical body.

When blood is extracted from the human body and coagulates, every particle is of a peculiar form not duplicated by the particles of any other human being. Therefore, the one who has blood of a certain person has a connecting link with the Spirit that built the blood particles. He has power over that person if he knows how to use this knowledge. That is the reason why Lucifer required the signature in Faust's blood, for with the *name* of his victim thus written in blood, he could hold the soul in bondage according to the laws involved.

Yes, indeed! Blood is a very peculiar essence, as important in white magic as in black. All knowledge in whatever direction used, must necessarily feed on life which is primarily derived from the extracts of the vital body: that is to say, the sex force and the blood. All knowledge that is not thus fed and nurtured, is as dead and as powerless as the philosophy Faust extracted from his books. No books are of themselves sufficient. Only in the measure that we take that knowledge into our lives and nourish it and live it, is it of real value.

But there is this great difference: that while the aspirant in the schools of the Sacred Science feeds his soul on *his own sex force* and the lower passions in *his own blood* which he thus transmutes and cleanses, the adherents of the black school live as vampires on the sex force of others and the impure blood drawn from the veins of victims. In the Castle of the Grail we see the pure and cleansing blood working wonders upon those who were chaste and aspired to high deeds, but in the Castle of Herod, the personification of voluptuousness, Salome, causes the passion filled blood to race riotously through the veins of the participants, and the blood dripping from the head of the martyred Baptist served to give them the power they were too cowardly to acquire through suffering, by cleansing themselves of impurities.

Faust aims to acquire power quickly by the aid of others, hence he contacts the danger point, just as everyone does today, who runs after self-styled "adepts" or "masters," who are ready to pander to the lowest appetites of their dupes—for a consideration—as Lucifer offers to serve Faust. But they can give no soul powers no matter what they claim. That comes from within, by patient persistence in welldoing, a fact which cannot be too often reiterated.

Chapter V

SELLING HIS SOUL TO SATAN *(Continued)*

BEING in a reckless mood, Faust answers contemptuously the demand of Lucifer for his signature in blood to the pact between them, with the following words:

> "Be not afraid that I shall break my word.
> The scope of all my energy
> Is with my vow in full accord.
> Vainly have I aspired too high;
> I'm on a level but with such as thou;
> Me the Great Spirit scorned, defied.
> Nature from me herself doth hide.
> Rent is the web of thought; my mind
> Doth knowledge loathe of every kind.
> In depths of sensual pleasure drowned
> Let us our fiery passions still;
> Enwrapped in magic's veil profound
> Let wondrous charm our senses thrill.

Having been scorned by the powers which make for good and being thoroughly inflamed with a desire for first-hand knowledge, for real power, he is ready to go to any length. But God is represented as saying in the prologue:

> "A good man in his darkest aberration,
> Still knoweth the way that leadeth to salvation."

Faust is the aspiring soul, and the soul cannot be permanently diverted from the path of evolution.

The statement by Faust of his purpose bears out the assertion that he has a high ideal, even when wallowing in mire—he wants experience:

> "The end I aim at is not joy.
> I crave excitement, agonizing bliss,
> Enamored hatred, quickening vexation.
> Purged from the love of knowledge, my vocation.
> The scope of all my powers henceforth be this:
> To bare my breast to every pang, to know
> In my heart's core all human weal and woe,
> To grasp in thought the lofty and the deep;
> Man's various fortunes on my breast to heap."

Before anyone can be truly compassionate, he must feel, as Faust desires to feel, the depth of the sorrows of the human soul as well as its most ecstatic joys; for only when we know these extremes of the human passion can we feel the compassion necessary for those who would aid in the uplift of humanity. By the help of Lucifer, Faust is able to learn both joy and sorrow, and thus Lucifer is indeed, as he says,

". . . The pow'r that still
Works for good, though scheming ill."

By the interference of the Lucifer Spirits in the scheme of evolution, the passions of mankind were aroused, intensified and led into a channel which has caused all the sorrow and sickness in the world. Nevertheless, it has awakened the individuality of man and freed him from the leading strings of the Angels. Faust, also, by the help of Lucifer, is led out of the conventional paths and becomes thereby individualized. When the bargain has been concluded between Faust and Lucifer we have the replica of the Sons of Cain, who are the progeny and charges of the Lucifer Spirits as we have seen in "Freemasonry and Catholicism."

In the tragedy of Faust, Marguerite is the ward of the Sons of Seth, the priesthood described in the Masonic legend. Presently the two classes represented by Faust and Marguerite are to meet, and between them the tragedy of life will be enacted and out of the sorrows encountered by each in consequence, the soul will grow wings that will raise it again to realms of bliss whence it came. In the meanwhile Lucifer conducts Faust to the witches' kitchen where he is to receive the elixir of youth, so that rejuvenated, he may become desirable in the eyes of Marguerite.

When Faust is presented upon the stage, the witches' kitchen is full of instruments supposed to be used in magic. A hell-fire burns under a kettle wherein love potions are brewed and there is much else which is fantastic. But we may pass by the inanimate objects without even mentioning them, and consider with profit what is meant by the family of apes which we find there, for they also represent a phase of human evolution.

Filled with a passion instilled by the Lucifer Spirits, or fallen Angels, mankind broke away from the angelic host led by Jehovah. As a consequence of the hardening power of desire, "coats of skin" soon enveloped them and separated them from each other. Egotism supplanted the feeling of brotherhood as the nadir of materiality was approached. Some were more passionate than others, hence their bodies crystallized to a greater extent. They degenerated and became apes. Their size also dwindled as they approached the line where the species must be extinguished. They are, therefore, the especial wards of the Lucifer Spirits. Thus the Faust myth shows us a phase of human evolution not included in the Masonic legend, and gives us a fuller and more rounded view of what has actually happened.

Once, all mankind stood at the point where the scientist believes the missing link to have been. Those which are now apes, degenerated from that point while the human family evolved to its present stage of development. We know how indulgence of the passions brutalizes those who give way to them, and we can readily realize that at a time when man was yet in the making, unindividualized, and under direct control of cosmic forces, this indulgence would be unchecked by the sense of selfhood which guards us in a measure today. Therefore, the results would naturally be more far-reaching and disastrous.

Some time the aspiring soul must enter the witches' kitchen as Faust did, and face the object lesson of the consequence of evil as represented by the apes. The soul is then left to meet Marguerite in the garden, to tempt and be tempted, to choose between purity or passion, to fall as Faust did, or to stand staunchly for purity, as did Parsifal. Under the Law of Compensation it will then receive its reward for the deeds done in the body. Indeed, luck is twin to merit, as Lucifer points out to Faust, and true wisdom is only acquired by patient persistence in well-doing.

> "How closely luck is linked to merit
> Does never to the fool occur.
> Had he the wise man's stone, I swear it,
> The stone had no philosopher."

True to his purpose to study *life* instead of *books*, Faust demands that Lucifer procure for him admittance to the home of Marguerite, and proceeds to win her affections by a princely gift of jewels smuggled into her closet by Lucifer. The brother of Marguerite is away fighting for his country. Her mother is unable to decide what is best to do with the gift and takes it to the spiritual adviser in the church. The latter loves the shining stones more than the precious souls entrusted to his care. He neglects his duty for a necklace of pearls, more eager to secure the gems for the adornment of an idol, than to guard the child of the church against moral dangers lurking around her. Thus Lucifer gains his point and quickly reaps a reward of blood and human souls, for in order to gain access to Marguerite's chamber, Faust induces her to give her mother a sleeping potion which results in the death of the parent. Valentine, the brother of Marguerite, is killed by Faust. Marguerite is cast into prison and sentenced to suffer capital punishment.

When we remember that the blood is the seat of the soul, and that it clings to the flesh of a person who meets a sudden and untimely end with the same tenacity as the kernel adheres to the flesh of an unripe fruit, it is easy to see that there is considerable torture connected with such a death. The Lucifer Spirits revel in the intensity of feeling and evolve by it. The nature of an emotion is not so essential as the intensity, so far as the purpose is concerned. Therefore, they stir the human passions of the lower nature, which are more intense in our present stage of evolution than feelings of joy and love. As a result, they incite to war and bloodshed, and appear evil now, but in reality they act as stepping-stones towards higher and nobler ideals, for through sorrow and suffering such as are engendered in the breast of Marguerite, the Ego rises higher in the scale of evolution. It learns the value of virtue by a misstep in the direction of vice.

It was with true appreciation of this fact that Goethe wrote:

> "Who never ate his bread in sorrow,
> Who never spent the midnight hours,
> Weeping, waiting for the morrow,
> He knows ye not, ye heavenly powers."

Chapter VI

THE WAGES OF SIN AND THE WAYS OF SALVATION

"THE wages of sin is death," says the Bible, and when we sow to the flesh we must expect to reap corruption. Neither should we be surprised that one who is negative of character, like the class described as the Sons of Seth, represented by Marguerite in the Faust myth, falls a prey to this law of Nature at an early date after his measure of sin has been filled. The speedy apprehension of Marguerite for the crime of matricide is an illustration of how the law works. The holy horror of the church that was remiss in not guarding her while there was yet time, is an example of how society seeks to cover up its negligence, and holds up its hands, shocked by the crimes for which it is itself, in a great measure, responsible.

Had the priest sought the confidence of Marguerite instead of coveting the jewels, he might have protected her from the fate that befell her, and though she might have suffered by losing her lover, she would have remained pure. It is, however, through the intensity of sorrow that the suffering soul finds its way back to the source of its being, for we have all as prodigal sons left our Father in Heaven; we have wandered afar from the realms of spirit, to feed upon the husks of matter, to gather experience and to gain individuality.

When we are in the slough of despair we begin to realize our high parentage and exclaim, "I will arise and go to my Father." Membership in churches, or the study of mysticism from an intellectual point of view, does not bring the realization of the *whither*, which is necessary before we can follow the Path. But when we are bereft of all earthly support, when we are sick and in prison, we are nearer and dearer to the Saviour than at any other time. Therefore, Marguerite in prison and under the ban of society, is closer to God than the innocent, beautiful and pure Marguerite, who had the world before her when she met Faust in the garden.

The Christ has no message for those who are satisfied and love the world and its ways. So long as they are in that condition of mind He cannot speak to them nor can they hear His voice. But there is an infinite tenderness in the words of the Saviour: "Come unto me all ye that labor and are heavy laden, and I will give you rest." The sinning soul symbolized by Marguerite in her prison cell, standing alone, ostracized by society as a moral and social leper, is impelled to turn her eyes heavenward and her prayer is not in vain. Yet, even to the last moment, temptations beset the seeking soul. The gate of hell and the gate of heaven are equally close to the prison cell of Marguerite, as illustrated by the visit of Faust and Lucifer who endeavor to drag her from prison and impending death to a life of shame and bondage. But she stands firm; she prefers prison and death to life and liberty in the company of Lucifer. She has thus stood the test and qualified for the Kingdom of God.

Solomon was the serf of Jehovah and as a Son of Seth he was bound to the God who created him and his ancestors. But in a later life, as Jesus, he left his former Master at the Baptism and then received the Spirit of the Christ. So every Son of Seth, must some day leave his guardians and take a stand for Christ, regardless of the sacrifice entailed thereby, even though life be the price.

Marguerite in her prison cell takes that important step and qualifies for citizenship in the New Heaven and the New Earth, *by faith* in Christ. Faust, on the other hand, remains with the Lucifer Spirit for a considerable time. He is a more positive character, a true Son of Cain, and though the wages of sin must eventually bring him death, salvation may come through a purer conception of love and through works.

In the second part of Faust we find the hero broken in spirit over the disaster which has befallen Marguerite through his instrumentality. He realizes his fault and begins to climb the road of redemption. He uses the Lucifer Spirit, bound to him by the bargain of blood as a means of attaining his end. He becomes an important factor in the affairs of state of the country whither he has journeyed, for all the Sons of Cain delight in statecraft as the Sons of Seth love churchcraft.

Not content, however, to serve another, under existing conditions, Faust sets the diabolical forces under his command to create a land, to raise it out of the sea and make a New Earth. He dreams a Utopian dream of how this free land shall be the home of a free people who shall dwell there in peace and contentment living up to the highest ideals of life.

These ideals are generated in his soul by the love of a character called Helen, which is a love of the loftiest and most spiritual nature, entirely separate from the thought of sex and passion. In the course of time he sees this land rise from the sea but his eyes are growing blind, for he is shifting his gaze from an earthly to a heavenly condition. While he thus stands looking at the forces marshalled by Lucifer, toiling at his behest day and night, Faust realizes that he has made real the claim of Lucifer, to be

"The power that still
Works for good though scheming ill."

He sees his work with the lower forces nearing completion, but his sight grows dimmer, and with that intense longing which comes to the soul to see the fruitage of its works, he desires to retain his sight until all shall have been accomplished and his Utopian dream shall have become a reality. Therefore, as the vision before him—the land rising from the sea and the happy people who live upon it in good fellowship—fades from his sightless eyes, he utters the fateful words named by him in his bargain with Lucifer:

> "Whenever to the passing hour
> I say, 'Oh stay! thou art so fair,
> Then unto thee I give the power
> To drag me down to deep despair.
> Then let my knell no longer linger,
> Then from my service thou art free;
> Fall from the clock the index finger,
> Be time all over then for me."

By the terms of that bargain, when Faust has uttered the fateful words the forces of hell are loosed from bondage to him, and he in turn becomes their prey: at least so it would seem. But Faust did not desire to stay the march of time for the purpose of enjoying sensual pleasures nor of gratifying selfish desires, as contemplated by the bargain. It was for the realization of an altruistic and a noble ideal that he wished to stay the passing hour. Therefore, he is really free from Lucifer, and a battle between the angelic forces and the hosts of Lucifer finally results in the triumph of the former, who carry the seeking soul to the haven of rest in the kingdom of the Christ, while they utter the following words:

> "Saved is the noble soul from ill,
> Our spirit peer. Whoever
> Strives forward with unswerving will
> Him can we aye deliver.
> And if with him celestial love
> Hath taken part, to meet him
> Come down the angels from above;
> With cordial hail they greet him."

Thus the Faust of the myth is an entirely different character from the Faust of the stage; and the drama which begins in heaven where permission was given Lucifer to tempt him, as Job was tempted in ancient times, also ends in heaven when the temptation has been overcome and the soul has returned to its Father.

Goethe, the great mystic, fittingly ends his version with that most mystic of all stanzas found in any literature:

> "All that is perishable,
> Is but a likeness.
> The unattainable
> Here is accomplished.
> The indescribable,
> Here it is done.
> The Eternal Feminine
> Draws us on."

This stanza puzzles all who are not able to penetrate into the realms where it is supposed to be sung, namely heaven.

It speaks of all that is perishable being but a likeness, that is to say, the material forms which are subject to death and transmutation are but a likeness of the archetype seen in heaven. "The unattainable here is accomplished"—that which seemed impossible on Earth is accomplished in heaven. No one knows that better than one able to function in that realm, for there every high and lofty aspiration finds fruition. The indescribable longings, ideas and experiences of the soul, which even it cannot express to itself are clearly defined in heaven; the Eternal Feminine, the great Creative Force in Nature, the Mother God, which draws us along the path of evolution, becomes there a reality. Thus the Faust myth tells the story of the World Temple, which the two classes of people are building and which will be finally the New Heaven and the New Earth prophesied in the Book of Books.

Parsifal

Wagner's Famous Mystic Music Drama

Parsifal

Chapter VII

PARSIFAL: WAGNER'S FAMOUS MYSTIC MUSIC DRAMA

AS we look about us in the material universe we see a myriad of *forms* and all these forms have a certain *color* and many of them emit a definite *tone;* in fact all do, for there is sound even in so-called inanimate Nature. The wind in the tree tops, the babbling of the brook, the swell of the ocean are all definite contributions to the harmony of Nature.

Of these three attributes of Nature, form, color, and tone, form is the most stable, tending to remain in *statu quo* for a considerable time and changing very slowly. Color on the other hand, changes more readily: it fades, and there are some colors that change their hue when held at different angles to the light; but tone is the most elusive of all three; it comes and goes like a will-o'-the-wisp, which none may catch or hold.

We also have three arts which seek to express the good, the true and the beautiful in these three attributes of the World Soul: namely, sculpture, painting and music.

The sculptor who deals with form seeks to imprison beauty in a marble statue that will withstand the ravages of time during millenniums; but a marble statue is cold and speaks to but a few of the most evolved who are able to infuse the statue with their own life.

The painter's art deals pre-eminently with color; it gives no tangible form to its creations; the form on a painting is an illusion from the material point of view, yet it is so much more real to most people than the real tangible statue, for the forms of the painter are alive; there is *living* beauty in the painting of a great artist, a beauty that many can appreciate and enjoy.

But in the case of a painting we are again affected by the changeableness of color; time soon blots out its freshness, and at the best, of course, no painting can outlast a statue.

Yet in those arts which deal with form and color there is a creation once and for all time; they have that in common, and in that they differ radically from the tone art, for music is so elusive that it must be recreated each time we wish to enjoy it, but in return it has a power to speak to *all* human beings in a manner that is entirely beyond the other two arts. It will add to our greatest joys and soothe our deepest sorrows; it can calm the passion of the savage breast and stir to bravery the greatest coward; it is the most potent influence in swaying humanity that is known to man, and yet, viewed solely from the material standpoint, it is superfluous, as shown by Darwin and Spencer.

It is only when we go behind the scenes of the visible and realize that man is a composite being, Spirit, soul and body, that we are enabled to understand why we are thus differently affected by the products of the three arts.

While man lives an outward life in the form world, where he lives a form life among other forms, he lives also an *inner* life, which is of far greater importance to him; a life where his feelings, thoughts and emotions create before his "inner vision" pictures and scenes that are everchanging, and the fuller this inner life is, the less will the man need to seek company outside himself, for he is his own best company, independent of the outside amusement, so eagerly sought by those whose inner life is barren; who know hosts of other people, but are strangers to themselves, afraid of their own company.

If we analyze this inner life we shall find that it is twofold: (1) The soul life, which deals with the *feelings* and *emotions:* (2) the activity of the Ego, which directs all actions by *thought*.

Just as the material world is the base of supply whence the materials for our dense body have been drawn, and is pre-eminently the world of form, so there is a world of the soul, called the Desire World among the Rosicrucians, which is the base from whence the subtle garment of the Ego, which we call the soul, has been drawn, and this world is particularly the world of color. But the still more subtle World of Thought is the home of the human Spirit, the Ego, and also the realm of tone. Therefore, of the three arts, music has the greatest power over man; for while we are in this terrestrial life we are exiled from our heavenly home and have often forgotten it in our material pursuits, but then comes music, a fragrant odor laden with unspeakable memories. Like an echo from home it reminds us of that forgotten land where all is joy and peace, and even though we may scout such ideas in our material mind, the Ego knows each blessed note as a message from the home land and rejoices in it.

This realization of the nature of music is necessary to the proper appreciation of such a great masterpiece as Richard Wagner's Parsifal, where the music and the characters are bound together as in no other modern musical production.

Wagner's drama is founded upon the legend of Parsifal, a legend that has its origin enshrouded in the mystery which overshadows the infancy of the human race. It is an erroneous idea when we think that a myth is a figment of human fancy, having no foundation in fact. On the contrary, a myth is a casket containing at times the deepest and most precious jewels of spiritual truth, pearls of beauty so rare and ethereal that they cannot stand exposure to the material intellect. In order to shield them and at the same time allow them to work upon humanity for its spiritual upliftment, the Great Teachers who guide evolution, unseen but potent, give these spiritual truths to nascent humanity, encased in the picturesque symbolism of myths, so that they may work upon our feelings until such time as our dawning intellects shall have become sufficiently evolved and spiritualized so that we may both feel and know.

This is on the same principle that we give our children moral teachings by means of picture books and fairy tales, reserving the more direct teaching for later years.

Wagner did more than merely copy the legend. Legends, like all else, become encrusted by transmission and lose their beauty and it is a further evidence of Wagner's greatness that he was never bound in his expression by fashion or creed. He always asserted the prerogative of art in dealing with allegories untrammeled and free.

As he says in *Religion and Art*: "One might say that where religion becomes artificial, it is reserved for art to save the spirit of religion by recognizing the figurative value of the mythical symbol, which religion would have us believe in a literal sense, and revealing its deep and hidden truths through an ideal presentation. * * * Whilst the priest stakes everything on religious allegories being accepted as matters of fact, the artist has no concern at all with such a thing, since he freely and openly gives out his work as his own invention. But religion has sunk into an artificial life when she finds herself compelled to keep on adding to the edifice of her dogmatic symbols, and thus conceals the one divinely true in her, beneath an ever-growing heap of incredibilities recommended to belief. Feeling this, she has always sought the aid of art, who on her side has remained incapable of a higher evolution so long as she must present that alleged reality to the worshiper, in the form of fetishes and idols, whereas she could only fulfill her true vocation when, by an ideal presentment of the allegorical figure, she led to an apprehension of its inner kernel— the truth ineffably divine.''

Turning to a consideration of the drama of Parsifal we find that the opening scene is laid in the grounds of the Castle of Mount Salvat. This is a place of peace, where all life is sacred; the animals and birds are tame, for, like all really holy men, the knights are harmless, killing neither to eat nor for sport. They apply the maxim, "Live and let live," to all living creatures.

It is dawn, and we see Gurnemanz, the oldest of the Grail Knights, with two young squires under a tree

They have just awakened from their night's rest, and in the distance they spy Kundry coming galloping on a wild steed. In Kundry we see a creature of two existences, one as servitor of the Grail, willing and anxious to further the interests of the Grail Knights by all means within her power; this seems to be her real nature. In the other existence she is the unwilling slave of the magician Klingsor and is forced by him to tempt and harass the Grail Knights whom she longs to serve. The gate from one existence to the other is "sleep," and she is bound to serve him who finds and wakes her. When Gurnemanz finds her she is the willing servitor of the Grail, but when Klingsor evokes her by his evil spells he is entitled to her services whether she will or not.

In the first act she is clothed in a robe of snake skins, symbolical of the doctrine of rebirth, for as the snake sheds its skin, coat after coat, which it exudes from itself, so the Ego in its evolutionary pilgrimage emanates from itself one body after another, shedding each vehicle as the snake sheds its skin, when it has become hard, set and crystallized so that it has lost its efficiency. This idea is also coupled with the teachings of the Law of Consequence, which brings to us as reapings whatever we sow, in Gurnemanz's answer to the young squire's avowal of distrust in Kundry:

> Under a curse she well may be
> From some past life we do not see,
> Seeking from sin to loose the fetter,

By deeds for which we fare the better.
Surely 'tis good she follows thus,
Helping herself while serving us.

When Kundry comes on the scene she pulls from her bosom a phial which she says she has brought from Araby and which she hopes will be a balm for the wound in the side of Amfortas, the King of the Grail, which causes him unspeakable suffering and which cannot heal. The suffering king is then carried onto the stage, reclining on a couch. He is on his way to his daily bath in the near-by lake, where two swans swim and make the waters into a healing lotion which assuages his dreadful sufferings. Amfortas thanks Kundry, but expresses the opinion that there is no relief for him till the deliverer has come, of whom the Grail has prophesied, "a virgin fool, by pity enlightened." But Amfortas thinks death will come before deliverance.

Amfortas is carried out, and four of the young squires crowd around Gurnemanz and ask him to tell them the story of the Grail and of Amfortas' wound. They all recline beneath the tree, and Gurnemanz begins:

"On the night when our Lord and Saviour, Christ Jesus, ate the Last Supper with his disciples He drank the wine from a certain chalice, and that was later used by Joseph of Arimathea to catch the lifeblood which flowed from the wound in the Redeemer's side. He also kept the bloody lance wherewith the wound was inflicted, and carried these relics with him through many perils and persecutions. At last they were taken in charge by Angels, who guarded them until one night a mystic messenger sent from God appeared and bade Titurel, Amfortas' father, build a castle for the reception and safe-keeping of these relics. Thus the Castle of Mount Salvat was built *on a high mountain,* and the relics lodged there under the guardianship of Titurel with a band of holy and chaste knights whom he had drawn around him. It became a center whence mighty spiritual influences went forth to the outside world.

"But there lived in yonder heathen vale a black knight who was not chaste, yet desired to become a Knight of the Grail, and to that end he mutilated himself. He deprived himself of the ability to gratify his passion, but the passion remained. King Titurel saw his heart filled with black desire, and refused him admittance. Klingsor then swore that if he could not serve the Grail, the Grail should serve him. He built a castle with a magic garden and populated it with maidens of ravishing beauty, who emitted an odor like flowers, and these waylaid the Knights of the Grail (who must pass the castle when leaving or returning to Mount Salvat) ensnaring them to betray their trust and violate their vows of chastity. Thus they became the prisoners of Klingsor and but few remained as defenders of the Grail.

"In the meantime Titurel had turned the wardenship of the Grail over to his son Amfortas and the latter, seeing the serious havoc wrought by Klingsor, determined to go out to meet and to do battle with him. To that end he took with him the holy spear.

"The wily Klingsor did not meet Amfortas in person, but evoked Kundry and transformed her from the hideous creature who appeared as the servitor of the Grail to a woman of transcendent beauty. Under Klingsor's spell she met and tempted Amfortas, who yielded and sank into her arms, letting go his hold upon the sacred spear. Klingsor then appeared, grasped the spear, inflicted a wound upon the defenseless Amfortas, and but for the heroic efforts of Gurnemanz he would have carried Amfortas a prisoner to his magic castle. He has the holy spear, however, and the king is crippled with suffering, for the wound will not heal."

The young squires spring up, fired with ardor, vowing that they will conquer Klingsor and restore the spear. Gurnemanz sadly shakes his head, saying that the task is beyond them, but reiterates the prophecy that the redemption shall be accomplished by a "pure fool, by pity enlightened."

Now cries are heard: "The swan! Oh, the swan!" and a swan flutters across the stage and falls dead at the feet of Gurnemanz and the squires, who are much agitated at the sight. Other squires bring in a stalwart youth armed with bow and arrows, and to Gurnemanz's sad enquiry, "Why did you shoot the harmless creature?" he answers innocently, "Was it wrong?" Gurnemanz then tells him of the suffering king and of the swan's part in making the healing bath. Parsifal is deeply moved at the recital and breaks his bow.

In all religions the quickening spirit has been symbolically represented as a bird. At the Baptism, when Jesus' body was in the water the Spirit of Christ descended into it as a dove. "The Spirit moves upon the water," a fluidic medium, as the swans move upon the lake beneath the Yggdrasil, the tree of life of Norse mythology, or upon the waters of the lake in the legend of the Grail. The bird is therefore a direct representation of highest spiritual influence and well may the knights sorrow at the loss. Truth is many sided. There are at least seven valid interpretations to each myth, one for each world, and looked at from the material, literal side, the compassion engendered in Parsifal and the breaking of his bow mark a definite step in the higher life. No one can be truly compassionate and a helper in evolution while he kills to eat, either in person or by proxy. *The harmless life is an absolute essential prerequisite to the helpful life.*

Gurnemanz then commences to question him about himself: who he is, and how he came to Mount Salvat. Parsifal displays the most surprising ignorance. To all questions he answers, "I do not know." At last Kundry speaks up and says: "I can tell you who he is. His father was the noble Gamuret, a prince among men, who died fighting in Arabia while this child was yet in the womb of his mother, Lady Herzleide. With his last, dying breath his father named him Parsifal, the pure fool. Fearing that he would grow up to learn the art of war and be taken from her, his mother brought him up in a dense forest in ignorance of weapons and warfare."

Here Parsifal chimes in: "Yes, and one day I saw some men on shapely beasts; I wanted to be like them, so I followed them for many days till at last I came here and I had to fight many manlike monsters."

In this story we have an excellent picture of the soul's search for the realities of life. Gamuret and Parsifal are different phases of the life of the soul. Gamuret is the man of the world, but in time he became wedded to Herzleide, heart affliction, in other words. He meets sorrow and dies to the world, as all of us do who have come into the higher life. While the bark of life floats on summer seas and our existence seems one grand, sweet song there is no incentive to turn to the higher; every fibre in our bodies cries, "This is good enough for me," but when the billows of adversity roar around us and each succeeding wave threatens to engulf us, then we have wedded heart affliction and become men of sorrows, and are ready to be born as Parsifal, the pure fool or the soul who has forgotten the wisdom of the world and is seeking for the higher life. So long as a man is seeking to accumulate money or to have a good time, so miscalled, he is wise with the wisdom of the world; but when he sets his face toward the things of the Spirit, he becomes a fool in the eyes of the world. He forgets all about his past life and leaves his sorrows behind him, as Parsifal left Herzleide, and we are told that she died when Parsifal did not return to her. So sorrow dies when it has given birth to the aspiring soul that flees from the world; he may be in the world to perform his duty but is not of the world.

Gurnemanz has now become imbued with the idea that Parsifal is to be the deliverer of Amfortas and takes him along to the Grail Castle. And to Parsifal's question, "Who is the Grail?" he answers:

> That tell we not; but if thou hast of Him been bidden,
> From thee the truth will not stay hidden.
> Methinks thy face I rightly knew.
> The land to Him no path leads through,
> And search but severs from Him wider,
> When He Himself is not its guider.

Here we find Wagner bringing us back into pre-Christian times, for before the advent of Christ, Initiation was not free to "whosoever will" seek in the proper manner, but was reserved for certain chosen ones such as the Brahmins and the Levites, who were given special privileges in return for being dedicated to the temple service. The coming of Christ, however, wrought certain definite changes in the constitution of mankind, so now all are capable of entering the pathway of Initiation. Indeed, it had to be so when international marriages took away caste.

At the Castle of the Grail, Amfortas is being importuned on all sides to perform the sacred rite of the Grail service, to uncover the holy chalice that the sight of it may renew the ardor of the knights and spur them on to deeds of spiritual service; but he shrinks, from fear of the pain the sight will cause him to feel. The wound in his side always starts to bleed afresh at the sight of the Grail, as the wound of remorse pains us all when we have sinned against our ideal. At last, however, he yields to the combined entreaties of his father and the knights. He performs the holy rite, though the while he suffers the most excruciating agony, and Parsifal, who stands in a corner, *feels sympathetically the same pain,* without realizing why, and when Gurnemanz eagerly asks him after the ceremony what he saw, he remains dumb and is thrust out of the castle by the angry, because disappointed, old knight.

The feelings and emotions unchecked by knowledge are fruitful sources of temptation. The very harmlessness and guilelessness of the aspiring soul renders it often an easy prey to sin. It is necessary to soul growth that these temptations come in order to bring out our weak points. If we fall, we suffer as did Amfortas, but the pain evolves conscience and gives abhorrence of sin. It makes us strong against temptation. Every child is *innocent* because it has not been tempted, but only when we have been tempted and have remained pure, or when we have fallen, repented and reformed are we *virtuous*. Therefore Parsifal must be tempted.

In the second act we see Klingsor in the act of evoking Kundry, for he has spied Parsifal coming towards his castle, and he fears him more than all who have come before, *because he is a fool*. A worldly-wise man is easily entrapped by the snares of the flower girls, but Parsifal's guilelessness protects him, and when the flower girls cluster around him he innocently asks, "Are you flowers? You smell so sweet." Against him the superior wiles of Kundry are necessary, and though she pleads, protests and rebels, she is forced to tempt Parsifal, and to that end she appears as a woman of superb beauty, calling Parsifal by name. That name stirs in his breast memories of his childhood, his mother's love, and Kundry beckons him to her side and commences to subtly work upon his feelings by recalling to his memory visions of his mother's love and the sorrow she felt at his departure, which ended her life. Then she tells him of the other love, which may compensate him, of the love of man for woman, and at last imprints upon his lips a long, fervent and passionate kiss.

Then there was silence, deep and terrible, as if the destiny of the whole world hung in the balance at that fervent kiss, and as she holds him in her arms his face undergoes a gradual change and becomes drawn with pain. Suddenly he springs up as if that kiss had stung his being into a new pain, the lines on his pallid face become more intense, and both hands are clasped tightly against his throbbing heart as if to stifle some awful agony—the Grail cup appears before his vision, and then Amfortas in the same dreadful agony, and at last he cries out: "Amfortas, oh, Amfortas! I know it now—the spear wound in thy side—it burns my heart, it sears my very soul. * * * O grief! O misery! Anguish beyond words! the wound is bleeding here in my own side!"

Then again, in the same awful strain: "Nay, this is not the spear wound in my side, for this is fire and flame within my heart that sways my senses in delirium, the awful madness of tormenting love. * * * Now do I know how all the world is stirred, tossed, convulsed and often lost in shame by the terrific passions of the heart."

Kundry again tempts him: "If this one kiss has brought you so much knowledge, how much more will be yours if you yield to my love, if only for an hour?"

But there is no hesitation now; Parsifal has awakened; he knows right from wrong, and he replies: "Eternity were lost to both of us if I yielded to you even for one short hour; but I will save you and also deliver you from the curse of passion, for *the love that burns within you is only sensual, and between that and the true love of pure hearts there yawns an abyss like that between heaven and hell.*"

When Kundry at last must confess herself foiled

she bursts out in great anger. She calls upon Klingsor to help, and he appears with the holy spear, which he hurls against Parsifal. But he is pure and harmless, so nothing can hurt him. The spear floats harmlessly above his head. He grasps it, makes the sign of the cross with it and Klingsor's castle and magic garden sink into ruins.

The third act opens on Good Friday many years after. A travel stained warrier, clad in black mail, enters the grounds of Mount Salvat, where Gurnemanz lives in a hut. He takes off his helmet and places a spear against a nearby rock and kneels down in prayer. Gurnemanz coming in with Kundry, whom he had just found asleep in a thicket, recognizes Parsifal with the holy spear and, overjoyed, welcomes him, asking whence he comes.

He had asked the same question on Parsifal's first visit and the answer had been: "I do not know." But this time it is very different, for Parsifal answers: "Through search and suffering I came." The first occasion depicts one of the glimpses the soul gets of the realities of the higher life, but the second is the conscious attainment to a higher level of spiritual activity by the man, who has developed by sorrow and suffering, and Parsifal goes on to tell how he was often sorely beset by enemies, and might have saved himself by using the spear, but refrained because it was an instrument of healing and not for hurt. The spear is the spiritual power which comes to the pure heart and life, but is *only to be used for unselfish purposes;* impurity and passion cause its loss, as was the case with Amfortas. Though the man who possesses it may upon occasion use it to feed five thousand hungry people he may not turn a single stone to bread to appease his own hunger, and though he may use it to stay the blood that flows from the severed ear of a captor, he may not use it to stay the lifeblood that flows from his own side. It was ever said of such: "Others he saved; himself he could not (or would not) save."

Parsifal and Gurnemanz go into the Grail Castle, where Amfortas is being importuned to perform the sacred rite, but refuses in order to save himself the pain entailed in viewing the Holy Grail; baring his breast he implores his followers to kill him. At this moment Parsifal steps up to him and touches the wound with the lance, causing it to heal. He dethrones Amfortas, however, and takes to himself the wardership of the Holy Grail and Sacred Lance. Only those who have the most perfect unselfishness, coupled with the nicest discrimination, are fit to have the spiritual power symbolized by the spear. Amfortas would have used it to attack and hurt an enemy. Parsifal would not even use it in self-defense. *Therefore he is able to heal,* while Amfortas fell into the pit he had dug for Klingsor.

In the last act Kundry, who represents the lower nature, says but one word: *Service.* She helps Parsifal, the Spirit, to attain by her perfect service. In the first act she went to *sleep* when Parsifal visited the Grail. At that stage the Spirit cannot soar heavenward except when the body has been left asleep or dies. But in the last act Kundry, the body, goes to the Grail Castle also, for it is dedicated to the higher self, and when the Spirit as Parsifal has attained, he has reached the stage of liberation spoken of in Revelation: "Him that overcometh will I make a pillar in the house of my God: he shall go out thence no more." Such a one will work for humanity from the higher worlds; he needs no physical body any more; he is beyond the Law of Rebirth, and therefore Kundry dies.

Oliver Wendell Holmes, in his beautiful poem, "The Chambered Nautilus," has embodied in verse this idea of constant progression in gradually improving vehicles, and final liberation. The nautilus builds its spiral shell in chambered sections, constantly leaving the smaller ones, which it has outgrown, for the one last built.

> Year after year beheld the silent toil
> That spread his lustrous coil;
> Still, as the spiral grew,
> He left the past year's dwelling for the new,
> Stole with soft step its shining archway through,
> Built up its idle door,
> Stretched in his last found home, he knew the
>   old no more.
>
> Thanks for the heavenly message brought by thee,
> Child of the wandering sea,

Cast from her lap forlorn,
From thy dead lips a clearer note is born
Than ever Triton blew from wreathed horn!
While on mine ear it rings,
Through the deep caves of thought I hear a voice
    that sings:

Build thee more stately mansions, O my soul!
As the swift seasons roll
Leave thy low-vaulted past,
Let each new temple, nobler than the last,
Shut thee from heaven with a dome more vast,
Till thou at length art free,
Leaving thine outgrown shell by life's unresting
    sea!

The Ring of the Niebelung

The Rhine Maidens

The Ring of the Niebelung

Chapter VIII

THE RHINE MAIDENS

REPETITION is the keynote of the vital body and the extract of the vital body is the intellectual soul, which is the pabulum of the Life Spirit, the true Christ principle in man. As it is the particular work of the Western World to evolve this Christ principle, to form the Christ within that it may shine through the material darkness of the present time, reiteration of ideas is absolutely essential. Unconsciously the whole world is obeying this law.

When newspapers start out to inculcate certain ideas into the public mind, they do not expect to accomplish this by a single editorial, no matter how powerfully written, but by articles of daily recurrence they gradually create the desired sentiment in the public mind. The Bible has been preaching the principle of love for two thousand years, Sunday after Sunday, day by day, from hundreds of thousands of pulpits. War has not yet been abolished, but the sentiment in favor of universal peace is growing stronger as time passes. These sermons have had but a very slight effect in so far as the world at large is concerned, no matter how powerfully a particular audience might be moved for the time being; for the desire body is that part of the composite man which was impressed at the time and was stirred thereby.

The desire body is a later acquisition than the vital body, hence not so crystallized, and, therefore, more impressionable. Because it is of a finer texture than the vital body, it is less retentive, and the emotions so easily generated are also easily dissipated. A very small impact is made upon the vital body when ideas and ideals filter into it through the auric envelope, but whatever it gets from study, sermons, lectures, or reading is of a more lasting nature, and many impacts in the same direction create impressions which are powerful for good or for ill according to their nature.

In order that we may benefit by this law of cumulative impacts, we take up for study, another of the great soul myths which throws light upon the mystery of life and being from a different angle, so that we may learn whence we have come, why we are here, and whither we are going more thoroughly than before.

As previously said, all myths are vehicles of spiritual truths veiled under allegory, symbol, and picture, and, therefore, capable of comprehension without reason. As fairy stories are a means of enlightenment to children, so these great myths were used to convey spiritual truth to infant humanity.

The Group Spirit works upon animals through their desire bodies, calling up pictures which give to the

THE RHINE MAIDENS

animal a feeling and a suggestion of what it must do. Likewise, the allegorical pictures, which are contained in myths, laid the foundation in man for his present and future development. Subconsciously these myths worked upon him and brought him to the stage where he is today. Without that preparation he would have been unable to accomplish that work which he is now doing.

Today these myths are yet working to prepare us for the future, but some are more under their spell than others. The path of empire and civilization has followed the Sun's course from east to west, and in the etheric atmosphere of the Pacific coast these mythical pictures have almost faded away, and man is contacting spiritual realities more directly. Further east, particularly in Europe, we find still the atmosphere of mysticism brooding over the land. There, people love the ancient myths which speak to them in a manner incomprehensible to the westerner. The soul life of the people among the fjords and fjelds of Norway, on the heaths and moors of Scotland, in the deep recesses of the Black Forest of Germany, and among the Alpine Glaciers, is as deep and mystical today as a thousand years ago. They are in closer touch with Nature Spirits and other fabled realities by feeling than we who have gone ahead upon the path of aspiration by direct knowledge. If we recall this feeling and combine it with our knowledge, we shall have attained an enormous advantage. Let us, therefore, try to assimilate one of the deepest mystical stories of the past, The Ring of the Niebelung, the great epic poem of northern Europe. It relates the story of man, from the time when he dwelt in Atlantis, until this world shall have come to an end by a great conflagration and the Kingdom of the Heavens shall have been established, as foretold in the Bible.

The Bible tells us of the Garden of Eden where our first parents dwelt in close touch with God, pure and innocent as children. It tells us how that state of being was abrogated and how sorrow, sin, and death came into the world. In ancient myths, like The Ring of the Niebelung, we are also introduced to mankind living under similar conditions of childlike innocence. The opening scene in this drama of Wagner represents life under the waters of the Rhine where the Rhine maidens swim about with rhythmic motion and a song upon their lips, imitating the undulating swell of the dancing waves. The waters are lighted by a great lump of lustrous gold and around this the Rhine daughters circle as planets move about the central Sun; for we have here the microcosmic replica of the macrocosm where the heavenly bodies move around the Central Light-giver in a majestic circle dance.

The Rhine maidens represent primitive humanity during the time when we dwelt at the bottom of the ocean in the dense, foggy atmosphere of Atlantis. The gold, which lighted the scene as the Sun illuminates the solar universe, is a representation of the Universal Spirit which then brooded over mankind. We did not then see everything in clear, sharp contours as we view objects around us today, but our internal perception of the soul qualities in others was much keener than it is now.

The individual Spirit feels itself an Ego and designates itself "I" in sharp contradistinction to all others, but this separative principle had not entered into the child men of early Atlantis. We had no feeling of "me" and "thee"; we felt ourselves as one great family, as children of the divine Father. Neither were we troubled about what we should eat or drink any more than children now-a-days are burdened with the material necessities of life. Time was to us one grand play and frolic.

But this state could not continue, or there would have been no evolution. As the child grows up to become a man or woman to take its part in the battle of life, so also primitive mankind was destined to leave its natal home in the lowlands and ascend through the waters of Atlantis, when they condensed and flooded the basins of the Earth. Evolving humanity then entered the aerial conditions in which we live today as told of the ancient Israelites who went through the Red Sea to enter the Promised Land, and of Noah, who left his native place when the flood waters descended.

The northern myth tells us the story in another way, but though the angle of vision is different the main points of the narrative bring out the same essential ideas. In the Garden of Eden our first parents did not think for themselves. They obeyed unquestioningly whatever commands were given them by their divine leaders, much as a child in early years does as its parents wish because it has no sense of self. It lacks individuality. This, according to the Bible story, was gained when Lucifer imbued them with the idea that they might become like the gods and know good and evil.

In the Teutonic myth we are told that Alberich, one of these children of the Mist (*Niebel* is mist, *ung* is child—they were thus called because they lived in the foggy atmosphere of Atlantis), coveted the gold which shone with such luster in the Rhine. He had heard that whoever obtained the gold and formed it into a ring would thereby be enabled to conquer the world and master all others who did not possess the treasure. Accordingly, he swam up to the great rock where the gold lay, seized it and swam rapidly towards the surface, pursued by the Rhine daughters who were in great distress at the loss of this treasure.

When Alberich, the thief, had reached the surface of the water he heard a voice telling him that no one could form the gold into a ring as required to master the world, save by forswearing love; this he did instantly and forthwith commenced to rob the Earth of its treasure and gratify his desire for wealth and power.

As said before, the gold, as it lay in its unformed state upon the rock of the Rhine, represents the Universal Spirit which is not the exclusive property of anyone, and Alberich represents the foremost among mankind who were impelled by the desire to conquer new worlds. They first became ensouled by the indwelling Spirit and emigrated to the highlands above; but when once in the clear atmosphere of Aryana, the world as we know it, they saw themselves clearly and distinctly as separate entities. Each realized that his interests were different from those of others; that to succeed and to win the world for himself, he must stand alone, he must look after his own interests regardless of others. Thus the Spirit drew a ring about itself and all inside that ring was "me" and "mine," a conception which made him antagonistic to others. Hence in order to form this ring and keep a separate center it was necessary for him to forswear love. Thus, and thus only, could he disregard the interests of others that he might thrive and master the world.

Alberich is not alone in his desire to draw a ring around himself for the purpose of gaining power, however. "As above so below" and vice versa, says the Hermetic axiom. The gods are also evolving. They also have aspirations for power—a desire to draw a ring around themselves—for there is war in heaven as well as upon Earth. Different cults seek to master the souls of men and their limitations are also symbolized by rings.

Chapter IX

THE RING OF THE GODS

BY appropriating a part of the Rhinegold, representing the Universal Spirit and forming it into a ring symbolical of the fact that it (the Spirit) has neither beginning nor end, the Ego came into existence as a separate entity. Within the confines of this auric ring it is supreme ruler, self-sufficient, and resents encroachment upon its domain. Thus, it placed itself beyond the pale of fellowship. Like the prodigal son, it wandered far from the Father, but even before it realized that it was feeding upon the husks of matter, religion stepped in to guide it back to its eternal home, to free it from the illusion and delusion incidental to material existence, to redeem it from the death incurred in this phase of the dense embodiment, and to show it the way to truth and life eternal.

In the Teutonic myth, the warders of religion are represented as gods. Chief among them is Wotan, who is identical with the Latin Mercury, and Wotansday or Wednesday, is still named in his honor. Freya, the Venus of Norway, was goddess of beauty, who fed the other gods on the golden apples which preserved their youth. Friday is her day. Thor, the Jupiter of the Norsemen, is said to drive his car over the heavens and the noise then heard is the thunder, and the lightning the sparks that fly from his hammer when he strikes at his enemies. Loge is the name of the god of Saturday. (Lorday in Scandinavian, a derivation from *lue*, the Scandinavian name for flame.) He is really not one of the gods, but related to the giants or nature forces. His flame is not alone the physical flame, but is also a symbol of illusion, and he, himself, is the spirit of deceit, sometimes currying favor with the gods and betraying the giants, at other times deceiving the gods and helping the giants to further his own schemes. Like Lucifer, the fiery Mars Spirit, he is also a spirit of negation, but delights also in obstructing life like the cold Saturn.

There is in northern mythology a reference to the still earlier cult wherein the deities of the water were worshiped, but the gods we mention superseded them, and are said to ride to the judgment seat every day over a rainbow bridge, Bifrost. Thus, we see that this religion dates from the dawn of the present epoch, when mankind had emerged from the waters of Atlantis into the clear atmosphere of Aryana—in which we are now living—and where they saw the rainbow for the first time.

It was said to Noah, when he led primitive mankind out of the Flood that so long as the sign of the rainbow remained in the clouds, the alternating cycles of summer and winter, night and day, should not cease, and the northern myth also shows us the gods gathered at the rainbow bridge in the beginning of this era. It and the gods remain until the moment when this phase of our evolution is ended, an event which will be shown to be identical with the description given in the Christian Apocalypse, which the Scandinavian myth will materially help to explain.

Truth is universal, and unlimited. It knows no boundaries, but when the Ego enveloped itself in a ring of separate vehicles which segregated it from others, this limitation made it incapable of understanding absolute truth. Therefore a religion embodying the fullness of pure truth would. have been incomprehensible to mankind and unsuited to help them. Hence, as a child who goes to school and learns a few elementary lessons the first year to prepare it for more complicated problems later, so humanity were given religions of the most primitive nature to educate them to something higher by easy stages.

Thus the warders of religion, the gods, are represented as desirous of building a walled fortress so that they may entrench themselves behind that wall and focalize their powers against the other faith. The Spirit cannot be limited without enmeshing itself in materiality; therefore, the gods, on the advice of Loge, the spirit of deceit and delusion, make a bargain with the giants, Fafner, and Fasolt, (representing selfishness), to build the wall of limitation. When that wall

THE RING OF THE GODS

surrounds the gods they have lost the universal light and knowledge; therefore, the myth tells us that part of their payment to the builders of Valhal was to be the Sun and Moon.

Furthermore, when religion has thus limited itself behind the wall of creed, the spirit of decay is introduced; it waxes old as a garment, and, therefore, it is also said that Wotan (wisdom or reason), agreed to give the giants, Freya, the goddess of beauty, who fed the gods on her golden apples to preserve their youth. Thus, by listening to advice from Loge, the spirit of deceit, the gods have sacrificed their light, their knowledge, and their hope of eternal youth and usefulness. Still, as already said, this was in a manner necessary, for mankind could not have grasped truth in its fullness then: we cannot understand it even now.

The spiritual power of religion is symbolized by the magic wand of Aaron in the Bible, by the magic spear of Parsifal in the Grail myth, and by the spear of Wotan in the story of the Niebelung. To bind the bargain with the giants, magic characters were cut in the handle of the spear, which was thus weakened, and in that manner it is shown that religion loses in spiritual power what it gains in material ways when it makes a bargain with the world rulers and panders to the baser appetites.

According to the teaching of the Norsemen, those only who died in battle were entitled to be taken to

Valhal. Wotan desires none but the strong and the mighty warriors. Those who died of illness or in peace upon their beds were condemned to the realm of hell, the underworld. In this also there is a great lesson, for none but the noble and the fearless who spend their days fighting the battle of life *to the very last breath* are worthy of advancement. The shirkers who love ease and peace, rather than the work of the world, are not entitled to promotion in the school of life. It does not matter where we work or what the line of our experience may be, so long as we faithfully battle with the problems of life as they appear before us. Neither will it suffice if we do this for a year or two and then lapse into inactivity; we must keep on working and striving until the day of life is done.

Thus the old Norse religion teaches the same lesson as Paul taught when he counseled "patient persistence in well doing." Even if we realize that we have not all truth, that we are placed under limitations by separateness, the egoism symbolized by the Ring of the Niebelung, and by creed and convention symbolized by the Ring of the Gods, still if we fill our appointed niche to the best of our ability throughout our whole life we shall be certain of advancement in a future age. We shall see more clearly through the veil of egoism when we willingly live the life where we have been placed, for the Recording Angels make no mistakes. They have put us in that place where we have been given the lessons needed to prepare us for a greater sphere of usefulness.

From what has been said, it is evident that the creedbound condition of the various churches—the insistence on dogma and ritual—are not unmitigated evils, as it may have appeared to many, but in reality the necessary outcome of the limitations incidental to the material existence through which the human Spirit is now passing, and thus each class is being properly taken care of. It receives as much truth as it can comprehend, and as is good for its present development. There is no need of worrying about anyone. No one can or will be lost, for, as in God we live, and move, and have our being, so, if one were lost, a part of the Divine Author of our system would be missing, an unthinkable proposition.

But while a great majority of mankind are thus being taken care of by the orthodox religions, there are always a few pioneers—some whose faculty of intuition tells them of greater heights unscaled, who see the sunlight of truth beyond the wall of creed. Their souls are starving on the husks of dogmas, and they long ardently for the apples of youth, and love sold by the gods to the giants. Even the gods are growing old rapidly, for no religion which is devoid of love can ever hope to hold mankind for any length of time. Therefore, the gods were forced to seek again the advice of Loge, the spirit of deceit, hoping through his wiles to extricate themselves from the dilemma. Loge tells them how Alberich, the Niebelung, has succeeded in hoarding up an immense treasure by enslaving his brothers. With the consent of the gods, he uses deceitful means to capture Alberich and forces him to disgorge all his treasures. He then plays upon the avaricious nature of the giants and finally succeeds in ransoming Freya.

Thus the curse of the Ring (egoism and selfishness) has tainted even the gods. For the sake of the Ring (power), Alberich, the Niebelung, forswore love. He oppressed his brothers and ruled them with an iron rod. Religion, on its side, forswore love by the sale of Freya. It also stooped to deceit to force the rulers of the world to pay tribute and when the Ring of the Niebelung passed into the hands of the giants the evil fate followed it, for one brother slays the other that he may be the sole possessor of the wealth of the world.

The gods have indeed regained Freya, but she is no longer the pure goddess of love. She has been prostituted; hence, she is but the semblance of her former self and fails to satisfy those whose intuition sees deeper than the surface; such are called Walsungs in the Scandinavian myth. The first syllable is the derivation of the German word, *walhlen,* to choose or the Scandinavian, *vaelge.* The last syllable means children. They are children of desire for free will and choice, who want to choose their own path and who seek to follow their own divine instinct.

Chapter X

THE VALKUERIE

"THE Valkuerie" is the name of the second part of Wagner's great musical drama, founded upon the northern myth of the Niebelungs, and the bearers of the name were children of Wotan, as were also the Walsungs.

The appropriateness of this name will be at once apparent when we understand that the mission of the Valkuerie was to go to battles whether fought between two or more, take the slain upon their horses, and carry them to Valhal. Therefore, a battle field or a place of combat was called *Valplads,* the place where Wotan, the god, chose the valiant ones who died fighting the battle for truth (as they saw it), to be his companions in the realm of bliss (as they conceived it). Brunhilde, the spirit of truth, was therefore chief among the Valkueries, the leader of her sisters, the other virtues. She was the favorite daughter of the god Wotan.

But when the gods had limited themselves and shut away the universality of truth by the Ring of Creed and dogma—symbolized by Valhal—the Walsungs, who are truth seekers first and foremost, rebelled. They manifest under different aspects as shown by the names given them in the northern myth. The root of their name is *Sieg*, a German word which means victory, and it is highly appropriate, for no matter what odds are against it, truth will win in the end.

Siegmund, the courageous one, who is impelled to seek truth no matter what the consequences, may be slain as the result of his audacity. We shall hear how and why, presently. Sieglinda, his sister and later his wife, who has the same inward urge but dares not openly follow it, may die in despair. She transmits the hunger for the truth to their offspring Siegfried, he, who through victory gains peace, so that what one generation of truth seekers fails to accomplish, will eventually be achieved by their descendants, and in the end truth will triumph over creed and stand supreme.

We are taking time by the forelock when relating or hinting at events which will be unfolded in the beautiful tale before us, but we cannot refrain from iterating and reiterating that glorious thought, "For now we see through a glass darkly." Though the walls and limitations of physical existence are about us in every direction, the time is coming when "we shall see and know even as we are known."

When Siegmund, impelled by the uncontrollable desire for truth, leaves Valhal, Wotan is enraged and in order to put a check on the independent spirit of the Walsungs, he orders the marriage of Sieglinda to Hunding, who is the spirit of convention. She swoons despairingly in his arms, for she has not the courage to leave her ancestors as her brother had done. Thus she is a fit symbol of those who, though they rebel in their innermost natures, are married to the conventions of the world and are afraid to make a radical change from the established code of the church, for fear of what people will think of them. Thus, though outraged in their innermost nature and thwarted in their holiest ambitions, they continue to bear the yoke of conventionality and go through the established church services for the sake of appearance.

In the course of time, Siegmund comes by chance to the house of Hunding and finds his sister whom at first he does not know, but when they have recognized each other, he induces her to flee with him. They both know that this act of theirs, this outrage against Hunding, the spirit of convention, will not be condoned by the gods, and to fortify themselves in the battle which they know is before them, they take with them a magical sword called Nothung. *Noth* is need or distress, and *ung* as we have already seen, means child. Thus the sword is the child of distress, the courage of despair. This sword had been buried to the hilt in Yggdrasil by no less a person than Wotan, himself, against just such an emergency as this. In order that we may thoroughly understand this beautiful symbol and the seemingly paradoxical conduct of Wotan, it will be necessary to elucidate the meaning of Yggdrasil, the World Ash, the tree of life and being, as explained in the Scandinavian mythology.

According to their concept, this wonderful tree reached from Earth to heaven. One of its roots was in the underworld with Hel, a terrible hag who ruled over those who had died of disease and were not, therefore, qualified to dwell with Wotan in Valhal. They represent the class of people who are indolent and neglect to fight the battle of life to the last. Hel has three children, who are closely akin to her and are always fighting the gods, who have the welfare of man at heart. They are symbols of the elements which make up the material world where death alone reigns. One is the Midgaard Serpent, a prodigious monster encircling the Earth and biting its own tail: it is the ocean. The other is the wolf Fenris, which is so subtle, yet so strong, that nothing can hold him: he represents the atmosphere surrounding the Earth and the winds which cannot be controlled. Loge, with whom we have already become acquainted, is the spirit of fire, deceit, and illusion. The other root of Yggdrasil is with the Frost Giants in chaos, whence this whole universe originated. The third root is with the gods.

Under the root, which is with Hel, the Serpent, Nidhog, lies gnawing. It is the spirit of envy and malice which is subversive of good: *Nid* means envy, and *hog*, to fell. Because Yggdrasil, the tree of life in manifestation, lives by love, envy and malice would fell the tree and bring it down to death and Hel. But under the root that is with the gods, is the fountain, Urd, whence the three Norns, or Fates, fetch the water of life—the spiritual impetus wherewith to water the tree and keep its leaves fresh and green. The names of these three Norns are Urd, Skuld, and Verdande. Urd is from the German, *Ur,* the past, primordial, or virgin state in relation to man and the universe. She spins upon her wheel the thread of fate generated by us in the past; and Skuld, a name signifying debt, is the second Norn, who represents the present. To her, Urd delivers the thread of fate of past lives which we must expiate in this embodiment. It is then given to Verdande, the third Norn, whose name is a derivation of *werdende,* the German word for becoming. She represents the future, and when the thread of fate symbolizing the debt paid at the present time is handed to her, she breaks it off piece by piece. Thus this wonderful symbol tells us that when the causation generated in past lives has worked itself into effects in this life, the debt is cancelled for all time to come.

The northern mythology further tells us that besides these three chief Norns, there were many others, and that one officiated at each birth and took charge of the destiny of the child then born. We are also told that these Norns, or Fates, did not work according to their own will but were subject to the dictates of the invisible Orlog. The name is a corruption of the word *Ur,* meaning primordial, and *log,* law. Thus we see the northern symbol teaches that the Norns were not subject to the gods, and that our destiny is not ruled by caprice but by an inexorable law of Nature, the Law of Cause and Effect.

Under the third root, which was with the Frost Giants, was the well of Mime. The Frost Giants, or nature forces, had existed prior to the establishment of the Earth. They had helped its formation and, therefore, knew many things which were hidden from the gods. Therefore, even Wotan, the god of wisdom, was wont to go to the well of Mime to drink therefrom, that he might receive a knowledge of the past. He also had to drink from the fountain of Urd that he might renew his life.

Thus we see that the Hierarchies, who help us to evolve, are themselves living to learn; and the very fact that they are learning shows their liability to err, and, also the reason why Wotan, their chief, should provide the sword, Nothung—the courage of despair—so that in an emergency those against whom he erred might have a weapon wherewith to defend themselves. Much more might be said about this wonderful World Ash, the Yggdrasil, but the student has now sufficient information to enable him to understand the relation of the sword to that which follows.

When Siegmund and Sieglinda, fortified with the magic sword—the courage of despair—leave the house of Hunding, the spirit of convention, to seek truth in the wide world, the outraged Hunding needs not the command of Wotan to pursue them with intent to kill. Wotan bids Brunhilde, the Valkuerie, to be invisibly present at the expected battle and fight for Hunding, the spirit of conventionality. But the spirit of truth cannot fight against the truth seeker, so Brunhilde sorrowfully refuses to comply with Wotan's orders. When Siegmund meets Hunding in deadly combat and is about to vanquish him, Wotan interposes his spear, and upon that the sword, Nothung, is shattered and Siegmund, defenseless, is killed by a blow from Hunding.

Thus truth is ever upon the side of the truth seeker in his battle against the conventionalities of the church and social customs. But when the power of religion, which furnished him the courage of despair necessary to stand up for his convictions, is pitted against the power of creed symbolized by the spear of Wotan, many an earnest soul has been vanquished, though not convinced. Siegmund may die, and Sieglinda may follow him to the grave, broken-hearted, when, assisted by Brunhilde she has given birth to Siegfried, the victor; for, as already said, the thirst for truth once felt can never be quenched until it has gained satisfaction.

In the meantime, Wotan powerless to abandon Valhal, the Ring of Creed, is forced to put away from himself Brunhilde, the spirit of truth, who has disobeyed him; for it is a condition of creed that it be autocratic and brook no gainsaying. But as all religions are inherently imbued by a spirit of love and a sincere desire to benefit and uplift mankind, Wotan feels an overwhelming sorrow at the step which is necessary for the continuance of the policy he has adopted, and which he adheres to despite the heart-rending pleadings of Brunhilde. It is a terrible thing to part company with truth, and both feel this more keenly than words can express, when the poor creed bound Wotan must perforce put Brunhilde to sleep, as he says: "Never to be wakened, until one shall come who is more free than I."

And in that saying he discloses the principal requirement in the quest of truth. "Unless a man leave father and mother," said Christ, "he cannot become my disciple." All limitations must have been swept away before we can hope for success in the quest of truth.

Chapter XI

SIEGFRIED, THE TRUTH SEEKER

WE have seen that it is necessary to set aside all limitations of religion, family, environment, and whatever else hinders in order to be able to grasp truth, but there is still another great requirement, or one which perhaps is comprehended in the first. We cling to our religion, our friends, and our families through fear of standing alone. We obey conventions because we fear to follow the dictates of the inner voice that urges us on toward the higher things which are incomprehensible to the majority; and therefore in reality, fear is the chief obstacle which prevents us from getting at truth and living it.

This is also shown in the Ring of the Niebelung. Wotan decrees that Brunhilde, the spirit of truth, is to be put to sleep, because he fears the loss of his power if he retains her after she has rebelled against his limitations and refuses to shield Hunding, the spirit of convention. He pronounces her doom in sorrow, saying that she must remain asleep until one more free than he, the god, shall waken her. "Perfect love casteth out all fear," and only the fearless are free to love and to live truth. Therefore, Brunhilde is put to sleep on a desolate rock, and around her burns forever a circle of flame kindled by Loge, the spirit of delusion. No one but the free—the unfettered and fearless soul—can ever hope to penetrate that circle of hallucination (conventionality) and live to love the reawakened spirit of truth, ever lovely and young.

Thus the second part of the mystic drama ends with the abandonment of truth, and the triumph of convention. Creed is firmly established on Earth. Siegmund, the truth seeker, lies vanquished and dead. His sister-wife, Sieglinda, also has paid with her life for entering the quest and it would seem as if Brunhilde must sleep forever. Now the Walsungs have only one representative, the orphan child Siegfried, who was left in the cave of Mime, the Niebelung, by the dying mother, Sieglinda.

In time, however, the child grows up in youthful vigor, developing the strength of a giant. Beautiful as a god, he is a strange contrast to Mime, the ugly Niebelung, a dwarf who claims to be his father. This Siegfried can scarcely believe, for when he looks about him in the forest, he sees that the nestlings resemble their parents, that the young of all animals have the same characteristics which are found in their parents. He alone is different from the one who claims him as a son.

When with prodigious strength he has caught a bear, and leads it into the cave of Mime, the latter is almost paralyzed with fear, an emotion utterly unknown to Siegfried. Mime, one of the most cunning smiths among the Niebelung, has forged sword after sword for the use of this young giant, but each in turn has been shattered by the powerful arm that wielded it. Mime has indeed tried to weld the sword Nothung, the child of distress, which was shattered upon the spear of Wotan in the fatal fray between Siegmund and Hunding. The fragments of this sword were brought by Sieglinda to the cave of Mime, but *no one who is a coward* can either forge or wield the sword, Nothung, the courage of despair; therefore, Mime, despite all his skill, has failed every time he has tried. One day when Siegfried taunts him because of his inability to make a sword that will stand, Mime brings out the fragments of Nothung, and tells him that if he can weld it, it will serve him well. Possessing that cardinal qualification of the truth seeker, fearlessness, Siegfried accomplishes with unskilled hand what Mime has failed to do. He forges anew the magic sword and is thus prepared for the quest of truth and knowledge.

Though ages have passed since Alberich, the Niebelung, was forced to part with the Ring as ransom to the gods, neither he nor his tribe have forgotten the power wielded by its possessor. And the longing to regain the lost treasure is still rife among all of them. For mankind, being inherently spiritual and free, will never be reconciled to the loss of individuality insisted upon under the regime of the church. Though, like Mime, they may be imbued with an uncontrollable fear; though they may cringe and fawn before the higher powers, as Alberich fawned before Wotan, they always, whether subconsciously or otherwise, remember their spiritual heritage and seek to recover their estate as free agents, unbound by creed or other limitations.

To this end they scheme and plot in the most subtle manner, as symbolized by the aid Mime gives Siegfried to forge anew the sword once shattered by Wotan. He sees that the young truth seeker is fearless. He knows that Fafner, one of the giants, who obtained the Ring from the gods, broods over his treasure in the form of a huge dragon, awe inspiring in the extreme. He can scarcely believe it possible for anyone to vanquish this monster, but he believes that if it can be done, this fearless young giant, Siegfried, is the only one able to accomplish the feat. It has, indeed, been said that the one who forges Nothung, will slay him; and Mime trusts to his cunning and hopes that if Siegfried kills the dragon, he, Mime, may be able to obtain possession of the Ring of the Niebelung and become the master of the world.

There is a very deep spiritual significance in this tale, namely, that of the lower nature, plotting to use the higher self for its own vile purposes. Siegfried (he, who through victory gains peace), is the higher self at that stage of its pilgrimage where it has been left all alone, without kith or kin, where it sees that the shape of clay symbolized by Mime is not part of it, but of an entirely different race and breed, where it is ready to continue its search for truth, attempted in previous lives as did Siegmund and Sieglinda, from whom the indomitable courage, that knows neither fear nor defeat, has been inherited.

But though the seeking soul may forsake the world, as did Hertzleide, the mother of Parsifal, who gave birth to the truth seeker in a dense forest, and as Sieglinda who bore the child, Siegfried, in the cave of Mime, the lower nature follows, scheming to use the power of spirit for worldly ends. Alas! how many have left the churches in despair because of creed, as Siegmund left Wotan; who have gained a certain knowledge of the higher things and have then misused their heavenly powers of hypnotism and mental suggestion, to attract to themselves the goods of this world, seeking rather the things of Earth which fetter than the treasures of heaven which free the soul.

There has never been an age on Earth when this part of the great myth was so generally enacted as it is today. There are many thousands of people who represent in themselves, Siegfried and Mime—Dr. Jekyl and Mr. Hyde. They are roused to a greater or lesser realization of the powers of the spirit, of their divine nature and attributes as Siegfried was, but the lower phase of their nature, Mime, keeps on scheming for material benefit.

And whether we call this use of the divine powers, Christian, or by an other name, it is not the science of the soul. We should be honest with ourselves and recognize the fact, that He, who had not a place whereon to lay His head, and who was the very embodiment of the attracting Christ power, refused to use that power for His own benefit. Even at the point of death He refrained, and it was said of Him that others He saved, but Himself, He could not (would not) save because the Law of Sacrifice is greater than the Law of Self-preservation: "For what shall it profit a man, though he gain the whole world and lose his own soul?"

The moment we set out upon the path in earnest, the lower nature is doomed despite all its efforts of cunning to save itself. And when Mime plans to send Siegfried against the dragon, Fafner, the spirit of desire, he has in fact sealed his own fate; for when the soul has conquered the desire for worldly possessions, we are dead to the world, even though we may still live here and perform our work in the world. We are then in the world, but not of it.

Led by Mime, Siegfried finds the giant Fafner guarding the cave where he has hidden the hoard of the Niebelungs. The lower nature always urges the higher to seek the material wealth of the world, seeking, thereby, to obtain standing and power in society. It is, alas, all too common, this desire and thirst for wealth and power! We are all like Mime, ready to risk our lives in the quest of gold. And though Mime quakes at the very thought of being near the dreadful dragon, he keeps on plotting, for he knows that when the Ego, represented by the Ring of the Niebelung, is so enmeshed in the snares of materiality that the body may be said to own it, when all its energies are directed by the lower nature, there is no limit to the power it may attain. But Siegfried, the fearless truth seeker, when he has vanquished the dragon, representing the desire nature, also slays Mime who is emblematic of the dense body.

Freed from the mortal coil, the Spirit is able to understand the language of Nature. Intuitively it senses where truth, represented by Brunhilde, the Valkuerie, is hidden, and following this intuition represented in the myth by a bird, he starts for the fire girt rock, to wake and to woo the sleeping beauty. But though we may, by laying aside the physical body, enter the realm where truth is to be found, the pathway is not by any means clear; for Wotan, the warder of creed, stretches his spear across the path of Siegfried, endeavoring to the last to dissuade or discourage the independent searcher for truth. However, the power of creed, represented by the spear of Wotan, was weakened when he bargained with the giants; in other words when it appealed to the lower side of man's nature. And in token of this weakening, magic characters were cut upon the shaft of the spear. This is therefore, easily broken in twain at the first blow from Nothung, the courage of despair.

When the truth seeker has come to the point here described, he will no longer allow himself to be thwarted in his quest, whether the opposing power be devils like Fafner or gods like Wotan. Every obstacle he removes with ruthless hand for he has only one desire in the world, an overweaning craving to know truth. Therefore, after shattering the spear of Wotan, he presses onward, led by the bird of intuition, until he comes to the circle of flame hiding Brunhilde, the sleeping spirit of truth. Neither is he daunted at sight of Loge's flames of illusion and hallucination. He plunges boldly through, and behold! there lies that for which he has panted during many lives. He stoops, gathers Brunhilde in his strong, yet tender arms, and with a fervent kiss he awakens the spirit of truth from her age long sleep.

Chapter XII

THE BATTLE OF TRUTH AND ERROR

THERE are no words adequate to convey a conception of what the soul feels when it stands in that presence, far above this world (where the veil of flesh hides the living realities under a mask) also, beyond the world of desire and illusion where fantastic and illusory shapes mislead us into believing that they are something very different from what they are in reality. Only in the Region of Concrete Thought, where the archetypes of all things unite in that grand celestial choir which Pythagoras spoke of as "the harmony of the spheres," do we find truth revealed in all its beauty.

But the Spirit cannot stay there forever. This truth and reality—so ardently desired by everyone who has been driven to enter the quest by an inward urge stronger than the ties of friendship, relationship, or any other consideration—is but a means to an end. *Truth must be brought down to this realm of physical form, in order that it may be of real value in the world's work.* Therefore Siegfried, the truth seeker, must of a necessity leave the rock of Brunhilde, return through the fire of illusion and re-enter the material world to be tempted and tried, to prove whether he will be true to the vows of love which pass between himself and the re-awakened Valkuerie.

It is a hard battle that is before him. The world is not ready for truth, and however vehemently it may protest its desire in that direction, it schemes and plots, by all means within its great power, to down anyone who brings the truth to its doors; for there are few institutions that can bear the dazzling brightness of its light.

Not even the gods can endure it, as Brunhilde knows to her sorrow, for was she not exiled by Wotan, because she refused to use her power on the side of convention! And anyone who steps upon conventionalities, to uphold truth, will find that the whole world is against him and that he must stand alone. Wotan was her father and he professed to love her dearly. Yes, he did love her in his way, but he loved the power symbolized by Valhal more. The Ring of Creed, whereby he dominated humanity, was more desirable, in his eyes, than Brunhilde, the spirit of truth; so he put her to sleep behind the circle flame of illusion.

If such be the attitude of the gods, what then may be expected from men who do not profess such high and noble ideals as the gods, the keepers of religion, were supposed to inculcate into them? All this and more than we can put into words—much that it will do the student good to meditate upon—flashed upon the mind of Brunhilde in the moment of her parting from Siegfried, and, in order to give him at least a chance in the battle of life, she magnetizes, as it were, his whole body to make him invulnerable. Every place is thus protected save one point on the back between the shoulders. Here we have a case analagous to that of Achilles, whose body was made invulnerable in all places save one of his heels. There is a great significance in this fact; for as long as the soldier of truth wears this armour, of which Paul speaks, in the battle of life, and boldly faces his enemies, it is certain that, however hard he is beset, eventually he will win. Because, by facing the world and baring his breast to the arrows of antagonism, calumny, and slander, he shows that he has the courage of his convictions, and a power higher than he, the power that is always working for good, protects him no matter how great the onslaught he faces. But woe be unto him, if at any time he turns his back! Then, when he is not watching the onslaught of the enemies of truth, they will find the vulnerable spot be it in the heel or 'twixt the shoulders. Therefore, it behooves us and everyone else who loves truth, to take a lesson from this wonderful symbology, and *to realize our responsibility to always love truth above everything.* Friendship, relationship, and all other considerations should have no weight with us compared with this one great work with truth and for truth. Christ, who was the very embodiment of truth, said to His disciples, "They have hated me, and they will hate you."

So let us not deceive ourselves: The path of principle is a rugged road, and strenuous is the labor of climbing. On the way we shall probably lose caste with everyone near and dear to us. Though the world now professes to grant religious freedom, the day of persecution has not yet ended. Creed and dogmatism are still in power, ready to prosecute and persecute anyone who does not go along the conventional lines. But so long as we face them and pursue our path regardless of criticism truth will always come out unscathed from the battle. It is only when we show ourselves to be cowards and cravens, that these inimical forces can give us our death blow through this vulnerable spot.

Another point: when Siegfried starts out from the rock of the Valkuerie to re-enter the world, he gives to Brunhilde the Ring of the Niebelung. This Ring, as you remember, was formed from the Rhinegold, representing the Universal Spirit, by Alberich the Niebelung. And we also remember that he could not shape this nugget until he had forsworn love; for friendship and love ceased when the Universal Spirit was surrounded by the ring of egoism. From that time the battle of life has been waged in all its fierceness: every man's hand being against his brother because of his egoism, which impels each to seek his own, regardless of the welfare of others.

But when the Spirit has found truth and has come in contact with the divine realities, when it has entered the Region of Concrete Thought, which is heaven, and has seen that one great verity—*that all things are one* and that though they may seem separate here, there is an invisible thread uniting each with all, when the Spirit has thus regained universality and love, it cannot be separate any longer. So, when it leaves the realm of truth, it leaves behind the feeling of separateness and self, symbolized by the Ring. Thus it becomes universal in its nature. It knows neither kin nor country, but feels like the much misunderstood Thomas Paine, when he said, "The world is my country; to do good is my religion." This attitude of mind is allegorically represented when Siegfried gives to Brunhilde the Ring of the Niebelung.

As you will remember, the Valkueries were daughters of Wotan, the chief god of the Norse mythology. They rode through the air on horses at great speed, to any place where deadly combat, whether between two or a greater number, was in progress. As soon as a warrior fell dead they lifted him tenderly to their saddles and carried him to Valhal, the abode of the gods, where he was resuscitated and lived in bliss forever after. You remember, also, that the name Valkuerie was interpreted as—chosen by acclamation. Those who fought the battle of life to the very end were chosen by acclamation to be the companions of the gods.

Brunhilde was chief of these daughters of Wotan, and her horse Grane, was the swiftest of the steeds. This animal, which had thus faithfully carried the spirit of truth, she gave to her husband; for *truth may ever be considered the bride of the one who has found it.* The horse, therefore, is symbolical of the swiftness and decision wherewith one who has married truth is able to choose aright and discern truth from error—only, *provided he remains faithful.*

Thus with the love of truth in his heart, and mounted upon the steed of discernment, Siegfried starts out to fight the battle of truth and bring the world captive to the feet of Brunhilde. Heaven and Earth hang in the balance, for he may revolutionize the world if he is faithful and courageous; but if he forgets his mission and becomes enmeshed in the sphere of illusion, the last hope of redeeming the world is gone. The *twilight of the gods is close at hand,* when the present order of things shall be done away, when the heavens shall melt in the fiery heat so that out of the travail of Nature a New Heaven and a New Earth may be born, wherein righteousness as a garment shall clothe all and everything.

Let us now turn our eyes from heaven, from Siegfried and Brunhilde, to Earth, where the world, which the truth is to set free, waits for the coming hero. The northern myth introduces us to the court of Gunther, a king honest and upright according to the standards of the world. Gutrune, his sister, is the highest lady in the land, her brother being unmarried. Among the courtiers there is Hagen, a name which means hook, signifying inherent selfishness. He is scion of the Niebelungs, related to Alberich who formed the fatal Ring. Ever since the days when that

Ring passed out of their possession, the Niebelungs have kept close watch upon its possessors: first, Wotan, who tricked Alberich and robbed him of the Ring, then Fafner and Fasolt, the giants who had built Valhal for Wotan, and who forced him to give them the Ring in part payment to ransom Freya, the goddess of love and youth, whom Wotan had prostituted and sold for the sake of power: then when Fafner slew Fasolt, the Niebelungs watched closely the cave where Fafner lay concealed, brooding over the hoard of the Niebelung as a huge dragon. And Mime, the foster father of Siegfried, paid with his life for scheming to obtain possession of the coveted treasure. Nor was Siegfried safe from their vigilant watch, save when he was at the rock of the Valkuerie; for no Niebelung, nor one who is a cur or coward, can ever penetrate beyond the circle flame of illusion into the realm of truth. Therefore, the Niebelungs do not know what has become of the Ring when Siegfried emerges anew into the world, though, of course, they surmise that it has been left with Brunhilde, and instantly commence plotting how to obtain it.

The court of Gunther lies directly in the path of Siegfried, and Alberich speeds ahead and informs Hagen that the last known possessor of the Ring is coming. Together, they scheme how to find out its whereabouts and obtain possession, but each in his black heart, also plots how to outwit the other and obtain the treasure for himself alone; for there is no honor in the battle of the separate self; each is against all others regardless of who they are. Though in the world we find co-operation for a common purpose, the question that is uppermost in the mind of every one who participates is: What can I get out of it? Unless this is plain and a personal reward is in sight, the great majority of mankind are unwilling to work. The apostle tells us, "not to be concerned with the things for self alone, but also, *to be mindful of the things of others.*" And we have given intellectual assent in the Christian countries, but, alas! how few are willing to live up to the ideal of unselfish service.

Chapter XIII

REBIRTH, AND THE LETHAL DRINK

"Birth is but a sleep and a forgetting.
The soul that rises with us, our life's star,
Has elsewhere had its setting,
And cometh from afar." —*Wordsworth.*

WHEN Siegfried leaves the rock of the Valkuerie and reaches the worldly court of Gunther, he is given a drink calculated to make him forget all about his past life and Brunhilde, the spirit of truth, whom he had won for his very own.

It is usually supposed that the doctrine of rebirth is taught only in the ancient religions of the Orient, but a study of the Scandinavian mythology will soon rout that misconception. Indeed, they believed in both rebirth and the Law of Cause and Effect as applied to moral conduct, until Christianity clouded these doctrines, for reasons given in *The Rosicrucian Cosmo-Conception* (p. 167). And it is curious to read of the confusion caused when the ancient religion of Wotan was being superseded by Christianity. Men believed in rebirth in their hearts, but repudiated it outwardly, as the following story told of Saint Olaf, King of Norway, one of the earliest and most zealous converts to Christianity, will show: When Asta, the Queen of King Harold, was in labor but could not bring to birth, a man came to the court with some jewels, of which he gave the following account: King Olaf Geirstad, who had reigned in Norway many years before and was the direct ancestor of Harold, had appeared to him in a dream and directed him to open the great earth-mound in which his body lay, and having severed it from the head with a sword, to convey certain jewels, which he would find in the coffin, to the queen, whose pains would then cease. The jewels were taken into the queen's chamber, and soon after she was delivered of a male child, whom they named Olaf. It was generally believed that the Spirit of Olaf Geirstad had passed into the body of the child, who was named after him.

Many years after, when Olaf had become King of Norway, and had embraced Christianity, he rode one day, as he often did, by the mound where his ancestor lay, and a courtier, who was with him at the time asked,

"Is it true, my lord, that you once lay in this mound?"

"Never," replied the king, "has my Spirit inhabited two bodies."

"Yet, it has been reported that you have been heard to say, on passing this mound, 'Here was I. Here I lived.'"

"I have never so said," returned the king, "and never will I say so."

He was much discomfited, and rode hastily away, presumably to avoid discussion of an inward conviction which all the dogmas of the new faith could not eradicate.

As a matter of fact, all ancient people, whether in the East or in the West, knew much about birth and death which has been forgotten in modern times, because second sight was more prevalent then. To this day, for instance, many peasants in Norway assert ability to see the Spirit passing out of the body at death, as a long narrow white cloud, which is, of course, the vital body; and the Rosicrucian teaching—that the deceased hover around their earthly abode for some time after death, that they assume a luminous body and are sorely afflicted by the grief of dear ones—was common knowledge among the ancient Northmen. When the deceased King Helge of Denmark materialized to assuage the grief of his widow, and she exclaimed in anguish "The dew of death has bathed his warrior body," he answered:

> " 'Tis thou, Sigruna,
> Art cause alone,
> That Helge is bathed
> With dew of sorrow.
> Thou wilt not cease thy grief,
> Nor dry the bitter tears.

> Each bloody tear
> Falls on my breast,
> Icy cold. They will not let me rest.''

Students, when they realize the fact of rebirth, generally wonder why the memory of past lives is blotted out, and many are filled with an almost overpowering desire to know the past. They cannot understand the benefit derived from the lethal drink of forgetfulness, and they look with envy at people who claim to know their past lives—when they claim to have been kings, queens, philosophers, priests, et cetera. There is, however, a most beneficent purpose in this forgetfulness, for no experience is of value in life except for the impress which it leaves by the purgatorial or heavenly post-mortem experience. This impress then acts in such a manner that at the proper time it directs, warns, or urges a certain line of action, and this warning, or urge, though dissociated from the experience, or rather for the reason that it is dissociated from the experience wherefrom it was extracted, acts with a quickness greater than that of thought.

To make this point clear we may perhaps liken this record, graven upon our subtler vehicles, to a phonograph record, which playing, will cause a battery of tuning forks placed near it to vibrate as each note is struck. From the outward point of view there seems to be no reason why a certain indentation on a phonographic record should correspond to a certain one on the tuning fork, and when the needle falls into that indentation, a definite sound should be produced which sets the tuning fork vibrating. But whether we understand it or not, demonstration shows that there is a tie of tone between that little indentation and the tuning fork. And this does not depend upon a knowledge of how the impress came to be imprinted on the record, or what caused the tuning fork to respond to that vibration. It is there, whether we know all the facts about it, or not.

Similarly, when we have had a certain experience in life, be it joyful or the reverse, it is condensed in the post-mortem experience, leaving an impress upon the soul to warn, if the experience is purgatorial; to urge, if heavenly. And in a later life, when an experience comes up similar to the one which caused the impress, the vibration is sensed by the soul; it awakens the tone of pain or pleasure, as the case may be, in the record of the past life, far more speedily and accurately than if the experience itself were called up before our mind's eye. For we might not, even at the present time, be able to see the experience in its true light while we are hampered by the veil of flesh, but the fruit of the experience, gathered in heaven or hell, tells us unerringly whether to emulate our past, or shun it.

Moreover, supposing we did really know our past lives: that by our present endeavors to live well and worthily we had acquired that faculty. Supposing that we had lived lives of debauchery, cruelty, crime, and selfishness! If people now despised us accordingly, we would then hold that they ought not to judge us by the past—that they were wrong in ostracizing us. We would contend that our present life of worthy endeavor should be made the basis of judgment, to the exclusion of former conditions, and in this we should be perfectly right. But then, for the same reason, why should we claim honor in the present life, adulation or admiration, because in the past life we were kings and queens? Even if it were true that we had held such positions, why should we lay ourselves open to the ridicule of skeptics by telling such stories? So, whether we have memory of our past lives or not, it is better to concentrate our efforts upon the highest possibilities of today.

There is no doubt, that one who is able to search the Memory of Nature, and who does so for the sake of investigation in connection with the progress and evolution of man, will, at some time or other, come into touch with glimpses of his or her own past. But a true servant who really feels himself to be a laborer in the vineyard of Christ, will never allow himself to swerve from the path of service and follow the trail of curiosity. The Disciple who receives instructions from the Elder Brothers, is warned at the first Initiation never to use his power to gratify curiosity, and on all subsequent visits to the Temple this idea is dinned into his ears.

The distinctions between the legitimate and illegitimate use of spiritual powers are so fine and so subtle, that, as one grows, the restrictions whereby one seems beset, multiply to such an extent, that, were the tale told to others, ninety out of a hundred would say: "But what is the use then of having spiritual sight or of being able to leave the body? When you are so restricted, it seems that the possibility of trespassing is multiplied to such an extent, that there is scarcely any use of having these faculties." Nevertheless, they are of great value, and the responsibility is only the natural result of added growth.

An animal takes freely anything that it wishes: it commits no sin and is not held responsible for its action, because it knows no better. But as soon as the idea of "mine" and "thine" has been imprinted upon our consciousness, then also the responsibility comes. As our knowledge grows, so does our responsibility; and the finer the soul qualities, the finer the distinctions between right and wrong. This we observe in our daily lives, that the standards of the permissible or non-permissible vary according to the quality of each individual.

And when we aspire to that power whereby we may know the past, we shall find that we are no more justified in using this power for aggrandizement, than we would be justified in using it to obtain worldly wealth or power. So the life, or the lives, we have led are hidden from us for a purpose, until we know how to unlock the door; and when we have the key we shall probably not want to use it.

For that reason, then, Siegfried is given the lethal drink the moment he enters the court of Gunther, and straightway he forgets about his past life with Mime, the dwarf, who claimed him as a son. He forgets how he forged the magic sword, "the courage of despair," which stood him in such good stead in the fight with Fafner, the spirit of passion and desire. He forgets that he had thus won the Ring of the Niebelung, the emblem of egoism, whereby he gained knowledge of his true spiritual identity and slew Mime, the personality, who wrongfully claimed to be his progenitor. He forgets how, as a free Spirit undaunted by fear, he broke the spear of Wotan, the warder of creed, and followed the bird of intuition to the abode of the sleeping spirit of truth. He forgets his marriage to her and the vow of unselfishness, implied when he gave her the ring.

But each and every one of these important events has left its impress upon his soul, and now it is to be tested: whether that impress has been deep or superficial. Temptation comes to us, life after life, until the treasure laid up in heaven has been tested and tried by temptation on Earth—whether or not it will withstand the moth of corruption. After the Baptism, when the Spirit of Christ had descended into the fleshy body of Jesus, it was taken into the wilderness of temptation to prove its weakness or its strength. And, similarly, after each heavenly experience we must expect to be brought back to Earth, that it may be learned whether we shall stand or fall in the furnace of affliction.

Chapter XIV

The Twilight of the Gods

WHEN Siegfried reaches the court of Gunther, Gutrune, the fair sister of the king hands him the magic cup of forgetfulness. Forthwith, he loses memory of the past and of Brunhilde, the spirit of truth, and stands a naked soul ready to fight the battle of life. But he is armed with the sublimated essence of former experience. The sword of Nothung, the courage of despair, wherewith he fought greed and creed symbolized by Fafner, the dragon, and Wotan the god, is still with him; also Tarncap, or the helmet of illusion, which is an apt symbol of what we in modern times call hypnotic power, for whoever put this magic cap on his head appeared to others in whatever shape he desired; and he has Brunhilde's horse Grane, discernment, whereby he, himself, might always perceive truth and distinguish it from error and illusion. He still has powers which he may use for good or evil according to choice.

As we have said previously, our idea of what truth is changes as we progress. We are gradually climbing the mountain trail of evolution, and as we do phases of truth appear which we never before perceived; and what is right at one stage, is wrong at another. Though, whenever we are in the flesh we see through the veil of illusion symbolized by Loge's flame which encircles the rock of Brunhilde, her swift charger Grane, discernment is also with us; and if we only give him free rein, the material brain mind, which is charged with the lethal drink of forgetfulness, can never gain the ascendancy over the Spirit.

The early Atlantean Epoch, when mankind lived as guileless "Children of the Mist" (Niebelung) in the foggy basins of the Earth, is represented in the Rhinegold. The later Atlantean time is an age of savagery, where mankind has forsworn love, as Alberich did, and forms "the Ring" of egoism, where it devotes its energies to material acquisitions symbolized by "the hoard" of the Niebelung, over which giants, gods, and men fight with savage brutality and low cunning, as set forth in the "The Valkuerie."

The early Aryan Epoch marks the birth of the idealist, symbolized as the "Walsungs" (Siegmund, Sieglinda, and Siegfried), a new race which aspires with a sacred ardor to new and higher things—valorous knights who had the courage of their convictions and were ever ready to fight for truth as they saw it, and to give their lives as forfeit to uphold their heartfelt convictions. Thus the age of realistic savagery gave place to an era of idealistic chivalry.

We are now in the latter part of the Aryan Epoch. The truth seekers of the past have again left the fire girt rock of Brunhilde. We have again assumed the veil of flesh and partaken of the lethal drink, and we are today actually playing the last part of the great epic drama, "The Twilight of the Gods," which is identical in its import with our Christian Apocalypse. "The gospel of the Kingdom" has been preached to us, "the Way, the Truth, and the Life" has been opened to us, as it was to Siegfried; and we are on trial now, as he was at Gunther's court, to see if we will live as "married to truth," or whether we will drag her from her retreat and prostitute her, as Siegfried did. In order to gain the hand of Gutrune, he wrested the emblem of egoism, the Ring of the Niebelung, from Brunhilde's hand and put it on his finger again; he bound her and carried her to Gunther to be his wife; he prostituted her, and himself committed adultery with Gutrune—for having once married truth, it is spiritual adultery to seek the honors of the world.

Heaven and Earth are outraged at this colossal betrayal of truth. The great World-Ash, the tree of life and being, shakes at its root, where Urd, Skuld, and Verdande, the past, present, and future, spin the thread of fate. It grows dark on Earth; Hagen's spear finds the only vulnerable point in Siegfried's body—his life is the forfeit, and as the highest ideal of the age has failed, there is no use in perpetuating the existing order of things. Therefore, Heimdal, the heavenly watchman, sounds his trumpet, and the gods ride in solemn procession over the rainbow bridge for the last time, to meet the giants in final battle involving the destruction of heaven and Earth.

This is a very significant point: At the opening of the drama we find the Niebelungen "at the bottom of the river." Alberich later forges "the Ring" in fire, which can only burn in the clear atmosphere such as we have in the Aryan age. During this age the gods also hold their sacred councils at the rainbow-bridge, which is the reflection of the heavenly fire. When Noah brought the original Semites through "the Flood," he kindled the first fire. "The bow" was then set in the cloud to remain for the age and during that time it was covenanted that the alternating cycles, summer and winter, day and night, et cetera, should not cease. In the Apocalypse (IV:3), John is offered instruction concerning "things which must be hereafter," by "One having a rainbow around Him"; and later (X:16), a mighty Angel with a rainbow on its head solemnly proclaims the end of time. Thus it is plain from the northern myth and the Christian teaching, that the epoch began when the bow was set in the cloud; when the bow is removed the epoch will end and a new condition of things physical and spiritual, will be ushered in.

THE TWILIGHT OF THE GODS 121

The other phenomenon attending this time of trouble is set forth in the ancient myth. Loge, the spirit of illusion, has three children: the Midgaard Serpent which encircles the Earth, biting its own tail, is the ocean which refracts and distorts every object immersed therein. Men fear the treacherous element; their cheeks have always paled at the thought of what it may do when unleashed. The wolf Fenris, the atmosphere, is also a child of illusion (optical), and the dread roar of the tempest may strike fear into the stoutest heart. Hel, death, is the third of Loge's children, and the "queen of terrors." Before man entered concrete existence, as described in the beginning of the great myth and in Genesis, his consciousness was focused in the spiritual worlds where the illusive elements, Loge (fire), Fenris (air), and the Serpent (water), are nonexistent; hence, death also was an unknown quantity. But during the present epoch when the constitution of the human body is subject to the action of the elements, death also holds sway.

At the sound of the trumpet of Heimdal, all the factors of destruction press forward to the plain Vigrid, the counterpart of Armageddon, where the gods of creed and their sworn supporters have assembled to make a last stand. The sons of Muspel (physical fire), press forward from the south, demolishing the rainbow bridge. The Frost Giants advance from the north. With an awful roar, Fenris, the tempest-driven atmosphere, rushes upon the Earth. So terrific is its velocity that the friction generates fire, hence it is said that its lower jaw is upon the Earth, its upper reaches the Sun, and fire streams from its nostrils. It swallows Wotan, the god in charge of the age of air, when the bow was in the cloud. The Midgaard Serpent or watery element is vanquished by Thor, the god of thunder and lightning, but when the electrical discharges have finally disposed of the element, water, there can be no thunder and lightning, hence the northern myth informs us that Thor dies of the fumes from the Serpent. In our Christian Apocalypse we also hear of thunders and lightnings, and are told that finally "there shall be no more sea."

But as the Phoenix arises rejuvenated and beautiful from its ashes, so also a New Earth, fairer and more ethereal, was seen by the ancient prophetess to arise from the great conflagration where "the elements melt with fervent heat"—"Gimle," she called it. Nor was it without population, for while the great conflagration was in progress a man and a woman called Lif and Liftharaser (lif means life) were saved and from them springs a new race which lives in peace and close to God.

> "A hall I see,
> More brilliant than the sun,
> Roofed with gold.
> On the summit of Gimle,
> There shall live

A virtuous race,
And enjoy blessedness
To eternity.
"Thither cometh the Mighty One—all—Father,
To the council of the gods,
In His strength from above.
He who thinketh for all,
Issueth judgments;
He causeth strife to cease,
And establisheth peace
To endure forever."

Thus the ancient northern myth teaches, but from a different angle, the same truths as found in greater fullness in the Christian Scriptures from Genesis to the Apocalypse, and it is important that we should realize the truth of these tales. There are, alas, too many in the class described by Peter as saying: "Where is the promise of His coming? For since the fathers fell asleep, all things continue as *they were* in the beginning." There are few who realize the import of the statement in the second chapter of Genesis, that "a mist went up from the ground and watered the earth before it rained," and that thus the children of the mist must have been physiologically different from the man of today who breathes air since "the Flood," when the mist condensed and became the sea. But just as sure as these changes happened in the past, so there is now another change impending. True, it may not come in our time—"that hour knoweth no man, neither the Angels, neither the Son," and repeatedly the warning of Noah is held up before us in this connection. In that day they ate and drank, married and were given in marriage, but suddenly the waters engulfed them and all who had not evolved the physiological requisites, *lungs,* necessary to live in the new condition perished. The Ark carried the pioneers safely through the catastrophe.

To make the next change safely, a Wedding Garment is required, and it is of utmost importance that we should work upon it. The same *soma psuchicon* or "soul body" which Paul mentions (I Cor. XV:44), is an etheric vehicle of paramount importance; for when the present elements have been dissolved in the impending change, how shall we survive if we can function only in a dense body as now!

The Germano-Anglo-Saxon race will of course be succeeded by two more before the Sixth Epoch is definitely ushered in, but today, and from our stock, there is being prepared the seed for the New Age. It is exactly the mission of the Rosicrucian Order, working through the Rosicrucian Fellowship, to promulgate a scientific method of development suited particularly to the Western people whereby this Wedding Garment may be wrought, so that we may hasten the day of the Lord.

Tannhauser

Pendulum of Joy and Sorrow

Tannhauser

Chapter XV

THE PENDULUM OF JOY AND SORROW

IN this drama we deal again with one of the ancient legends. It was given to humanity by the divine Hierarchies who guided us along the path of progress by pictorial terms so that mankind might subconsciously absorb the ideals for which, in later lives, they were to strive.

In ancient times love was brutal; the bride was bought or stolen or taken as a prize in war. Possession *of the body* was all that was desired, therefore woman was a chattel, prized by man for the pleasure she afforded him, and for that only. The higher, finer faculties in her nature were not given a chance of expression. This condition had to be altered or human progress would have stopped. The apple always falls close to the tree. Anyone born from a union under such brutal conditions must be brutal; and, if mankind were to be elevated, the standard of love had to be raised. *Tannhauser* is an attempt in that direction.

This legend is also called "The Tournament of the Troubadours," for the minstrels of Europe were the educators of the Middle Ages. They were wandering knights, gifted with the power of speech and song, who journeyed from land to land, welcomed and honored in court and castle. They had a powerful influence in forming the ideas and ideals of the day, and in the Tournament of Song held in Wartburg Castle, one of the problems of that day—whether woman had a right to her own body or not, a right to protection against licentious abuse by her husband, whether she was to be considered a companion to be loved as soul to soul or as a slave bound to submit to the dictates of her master—was the question to be decided.

Naturally, at each change there are always those who stand for the old things against the new, and champions of both sides took part in that battle of song in Wartburg Castle.

The question is still rife. It is still unsettled with the majority of mankind, but the principle enunciated is true, and only as we conform to this principle by elevating the standards of love, can a better race be born. This is particularly essential to one who is aiming to lead a higher life. Though the principle seems so self-evident it is not even yet agreed to by all who make high professions. In time everyone will learn that only as we regard woman as the equal of man can mankind truly be elevated, for under the Law of Rebirth the soul is reborn alternately in both sexes, and the oppressors of one age become the oppressed of the next.

The fallacy of a double standard of conduct which favors one sex at the cost of the other should be at once apparent to anyone who believes in the succession of lives whereby the soul progresses from impotence to omnipotence. It has been amply proved that, far from inferior to man, woman is at least his equal and very often his superior in many of the mental occupations; though that does not appear plainly from the drama.

The legend tells us that Tannhauser, who represents the soul at a certain stage of development, has been disappointed in love, because its object, Elizabeth, was too pure and too young to be even approached with a request that she yield to him. Yearning with passionate desire, he attracts something of an identical nature.

Our thoughts are like tuning forks. They awaken echoes in others who are capable of responding to them, and the passionate thought of Tannhauser brings him, therefore, to that which is called "the Mountain of Venus."

Like *A Midsummer Night's Dream* of Shakespeare, this story of how he finds the Mountain of Venus, of how he is taken in by this lovely goddess, and is kept in passion's chains by her charms, is not entirely founded upon fancy. There are Spirits in the air, in the water, and in the fire; and under certain conditions they are contacted by man. Not so much perhaps in the electric atmosphere of America, but over all of Europe, particularly in the north, there broods a mystic atmosphere which has somewhat attuned the people to the seeing of these elementals. The goddess of beauty, or Venus, here spoken of, is really one of the etheric entities who feed upon the fumes of low desire, in the gratification of which the creative force is liberated in copious quantities. Many of the Spirit controls which take possession of mediums and incite them to laxity of morals and abuses, who act as their soul lovers and seriously weaken their victims, belong to this same class which is exceedingly dangerous, to say the least. Paracelsus mentions them as "incubi" and "succubi."

The opening scene of Tannhauser introduces us to a licentious debauch in the cave of Venus. Tannhauser is kneeling before the goddess who is stretched on a couch. He wakens as if from a dream, and his dream has inculcated a longing to visit the Earth above again. This he tells the goddess Venus who answers:

> "What foolish plaint! Art weary of my love?
> By sorrow once thy heart was crushed above.
> Up minstrel, seize thy harp and sing of bliss divine,
> For love's chief treasure, love's goddess is thine."

Inflamed with new ardor Tannhauser seizes harp and sings her praise:

> "All hail to thee! Undying fame attend thee.
> Paeans of praise to thee be ever sung.
> Each soft delight thy bounty sweet did lend me,
> Shall wake my harp while time and love are young;
> For love's sweet joy, and satisfaction's pleasure,
> My sense did thirst, my heart did crave;
> And thou, whose love a God alone can measure,
> Gave me thyself, and in this bliss I lave.
> But mortal am I, and a love divine,
> Too changeless is to mate with mine.
> A god can love without cessation,
> But under laws of alternation,
> Our share of pain as well as pleasure,
> We mortals need in changing measure.
> Too full of joy, again I long for pain,
> So, Queen, I cannot here remain."

When mankind emerged from Atlantis, and came into the air of Aryana, the rainbow stood for the first time in the sky as the sign of the new age. At that time it was said that as long as this bow was in the clouds the seasons would not cease to change; day and night, summer and winter, ebb and flood, and all the other alternating measures of Nature would follow one another in unbroken succession. In music there may not always be harmony. Discord once in a while comes in to give appreciation of the melody which follows. Thus it is with the question of pain and sorrow, of joy and happiness: *they are also measures of alternation.* We cannot live in one without craving the other, any more than we could remain in heaven and gather experiences that are only to be found upon Earth. And it is this inward urge, this swing of the pendulum from joy to sorrow and back again, which drives Tannhauser from the cave of Venus that he may again know the strife and struggle of the world; that he may there gain the experience which sorrow alone can give and forget the pleasures which bring to him no soul power. But it is characteristic of the lower forces, however, that they always seek to influence the soul against its will; that they always use every endeavor to keep it away from the path of rectitude; and so Venus who stands as the representative of these powers in the drama of Tannhauser, warningly and dissuasively says:

The Pendulum of Joy and Sorrow 133

"In dust thy soul will soon be humbled,
   Adversity thy pride will fell,
Then crushed in spirit, ardor crumbled,
   Thou'lt plead again to feel my spell."

But Tannhauser is firm in his purpose. The urge within him is so strong that nothing can keep him back, and though he still feels the spell, he exclaims with great fervor:

"While I have life, but thee my harp will praise,
No meaner theme will e'er my song inspire;
Thou spring of beauty and of gentle grace,
With sweetest songs dost quicken love's desire;
The fire thou kindlest in my heart,
An altar flame will burn alone for thee,
And though in sorrow now from thee I part,
Thy champion I shall ever be.
But I must forth, the life of earth I crave,
Here I must aye remain a slave;
I thirst for freedom though my death it be,
Therefore, O Queen, from thee I flee!"

Thus when Tannhauser leaves the cave of Venus he is the pledged champion of the low and sensual side of love; and this he goes out into the world to teach, for that is the nature of mankind: *whatever the heart feels,* must out.

Knowing the country well, he at once turns his steps toward Wartburg where a number of minstrels are always staying with the lord and lady of the manor, who to a very large extent are patrons of minstrelsy always anxious to be entertained, and always lavish with their gifts.

After awhile he meets a band of minstrels who are walking in the woods, and these, his former friends, are surprised that they have not seen him for so long. They ask him where he has been, but Tannhauser, knowing that there is a general sentiment against being with the lower elemental forces in Nature, hides his whereabouts during the period of his absence from them, by giving an evasive answer. He is then told by the minstrels that there is to be a tournament of the troubadours at the castle and is invited to go with them.

Hearing that the subject of the song contest is to be love, and furthermore, that the prize will be given to the winner by the hand of the beautiful daughter of the lord, namely Elizabeth, (the lady Tannhauser has loved so ardently and who so inflamed his soul in past days that it drove him to the cave of Venus) he hopes by the ardor with which he is inspired, to induce the beautiful maiden to hear his plaint. As we always reap a harvest of pain whenever we go contrary to the laws of progress, Tannhauser, by this act, is sowing the seed that will one day bring him the harvest of pain he coveted in the cave of Venus.

Chapter XVI

MINSTRELS, INITIATES OF MIDDLE AGES

WHEN Tannhauser emerged from the cave of Venus one of the first sounds which greeted him was the chant of a band of pilgrims going to Rome to obtain forgiveness for their sins, and this awakened within him an overpowering sense of his own delinquency. Therefore he kneels and exclaims in deep contrition:

"Almighty, praise I give to Thee,
I pray Thee mercy show to me.
By sense of sin I am oppressed,
The load too heavy far for me.
I have no peace, can find no rest
Till pardon I receive from Thee."

While he is thus dejected and feels himself accursed, doomed to roam alone and unblessed through the world because of his unhallowed love for Venus, the minstrels come upon him, and recognizing him, endeavor to persuade him to accompany them to Wartburg, but as said before, it was the *passionate* love of Elizabeth that drove him thence, and he feels that he dare not approach her. As a last argument, Wolfram von Eschenbach tells Tannhauser that Elizabeth loves him. Elizabeth has never been at the contests of song since Tannhauser left, and Wolfram von Eschenbach, one of the purest and most beautiful characters in medieval history, endeavors to secure the happiness of Elizabeth by bringing Tannhauser back to her though he himself loves her, and it breaks his own heart to do so. On hearing this, *passion* fires Tannhauser's soul anew, and he sings:

> "Ah, dost thou smile once more upon me!
> Thou radiant world that I had lost!
> O sun of heaven thou dost not shun me
> By stormy clouds so long o'ercrossed.
> 'Tis May, sweet May. Its thousand carols tender,
> Rejoicing set my sorrow free.
> A ray of new, unwonted splendor
> Illumes my soul, O joy 'tis she!"

On meeting Tannhauser at the castle, Elizabeth tells him:

> "Now the world to me is darkened.
> Repose and joy from me have flown.
> Since fondly to thy lays I've hearkened,
> The pangs of bliss and woe I've known;
> And when this land thou hadst forsaken,
> My peace of heart had also fled.
> No minstrel could my joy awaken,
> To me their lays seem sad and dead.
> In slumber oft near broken-hearted,

Awake, each pang was oft recalled;
All joy has from my life departed.
Oh tell me why I am enthralled!"

To this Tannhauser replies:

"All praise to love for this sweet token!
Love touched my harp with magic sweet.
Love through my song to thee hath spoken
And captured, leaves me at thy feet."

Elizabeth then confesses:

"O blessed hour of meeting!
O blessed power of love!
At last I give thee greeting,
No longer wilt thou rove.
Now life anew awakens,
Within this heart of mine;
The cloud of sorrow breaketh.
The sun of joy doth shine."

Thus Elizabeth has inspired love in the hearts of two of the minstrels, Wolfram and Tannhauser, but how different this love is will be seen from the way each handles the theme in the contest of song, which follows in the second act, where the Lord of Wartburg opens the contest with the following words:

"As oft in war times, death we braved,
And knightlike battled, honor to maintain,
So, minstrels, you have fought and virtue saved.

> Upheld true faith with voice and harp's sweet strain.
> Tune up again; another lay indite.
> *Describe true love,* that we may surely know;
> And who so does most nobly this recite
> The princess shall reward on him bestow."

In this last verse we gain a true understanding of the relative scope and mission of knighthood and minstrelsy. It was the duty of knights to follow war, to defend with the sword all who were in need thereof, to fight with a strong arm the battle of the weak. In so far as a knight followed the code of honor then prevailing, and defended the weak, keeping faith with friend and foe, he learned the lessons of physical and, in a certain sense, of moral courage, which are so necessary for the development of the soul. Anyone who enters upon the path of spiritual attainment is also a knight of noble birth, and it behooves him to realize that he must have the same virtues which were required of knighthood, for upon the spiritual path there are also dangers and places where physical courage is required. The Spirit, for instance, cannot come to liberation without physical inconvenience. Sickness usually attends soul growth to a greater or a less extent, and it requires physical courage to endure the suffering incident to that attainment, after which we all strive, and thus sacrifice the body for the soul.

It was the mission of minstrelsy to foster this courage and to inculcate the finer virtues also. All min-

MINSTRELS, INITIATES OF MIDDLE AGES 139

strels, therefore, had that poetical strain which brings us in touch with the higher and finer things in Nature not sensed by ordinary humanity; but more than that, many among the minstrels in medieval times were Initiates themselves, or perhaps lay brothers. Therefore their words were often found to be pearls of wisdom. They were looked up to as teachers, as wise men, and were friends of the true nobility.

There were, of course, exceptions, but Tannhauser was not one of these, however. We shall find that he was really a noble soul despite his faults, and in fact we should remember that we are all Tannhausers before we become Wolframs. We all respond to Tannhauser's definition of love before we grow to Wolfram's spiritual conception as given at the contest.

Lots are drawn to see who shall begin the contest, and the name of Wolfram appears on the slip first taken from the box. He therefore commences as follows:

> "Gazing around upon this fair assemblage
> How does the heart expand to see the scene!
> These gallant heroes, valiant, wise, and gentle,
> As stately forests growing fresh and green,
> And blooming by their side in sweet perfection,
> I see a wreath of dames and maidens fair.
> Their blended glories dazzle the beholder,
> My song is mute before this vision rare.
> I raise my eyes to one whose starry splendor

In this bright heaven with mild effulgence beams,
And gazing on that radiance, pure and tender
My heart is sunk in prayerful, holy dreams.
And lo, the source of all delight and power
Is then unto my listening soul revealed.
From whose unfathomed depths, all joy doth shower
The tender balm through which all grief is healed.
Oh! never may I dim its limpid waters
Nor rashly trouble them with wild desires.
I'll worship thee, kneeling, with soul devoted.
To live and die for thee my heart aspires.
I know not if these feeble words can render
What I have felt of love both true and tender.''

At the end of Wolfram's song Tannhauser starts as if from a dream. He rises and sings:

"I, too, drank from that well of pleasure;
Its waters, Wolfram, well I know;
Who that has life may dare ignore it?
Hear how its virtues I will show:
But I would not draw near its margin
Unless desire consumed my soul;
Then only would its wave refresh me,
My life and heart make new and whole.
O tide of joy, let me possess thee!
All fear and doubt before thee fly;
Let thy unfathomed raptures bless me!
For thee alone my heart beats high,
So that I own thy fiery splendor,

> Let me with longing ever burn.
> I tell thee, Wolfram, thus I render
> What I have known of truest love.''

Here we have the true description of the two extremes of love; that of Wolfram being the love of soul for soul, Tannhauser's being the love of sense. One is the love that seeks to give, the other demands possession that it may receive. This is only the beginning of the contest, of which we shall hear fully later, but these being the definitions first given by the two chief exponents of love, it is well worth noting that Wolfram von Eschenbach stands as the exponent of the new and the more beautiful love which is to supersede the primeval conception.

Even to this day, unfortunately, the ancient idea is entertained that possession is the signature of love. Those who believe in rebirths in alternate sexes, should by this fact be sufficiently convinced that, as the soul is bisexual and our bodies contain rudimentary organs belonging to the opposite sex, so it is no more than proper and just that each human being regardless of the polarity of the present garb, should have the same privileges as the other.

Chapter XVII

THE UNPARDONABLE SIN

DURING the contest the sublime and heavenly ideals of the companionship of soul with soul, is sung by the majority of the minstrels, and at each presentation there comes from Tannhauser a passionate retort defending the sensual phase of love. At last, enraged at their seeming insipidity, which he regards as sentimental nonsense, he cries, "Go to Venus. She will show you love."

With this remark his guilty secret is out. It is taken by everyone to mean that he has committed that which is the worst phase of the unpardonable sin, namely, intercourse with an etheric entity; and feeling that he is depraved beyond redemption, they rush at him sword in hand and would surely have killed him had not Elizabeth interceded, pleading that he be not cut off from life in his sins, but be given a chance to repent. Then a band of pilgrims is heard in the distance and the minstrels agree that if he will go and seek the pardon of the Holy See at Rome, they will spare his life.

When Elizabeth reveals the grief of her heart in her plea for Tannhauser, he at last sees the enormity of his sins and is seized with an overwhelming sense of his depravity. He, therefore, anxiously grasps the suggestion given him, joins the band of pilgrims, and journeys toward Rome. Being a strong soul, he does nothing by halves. His contrition is as sincere as his sin was brazen. His whole being yearns to cleanse itself from impurity that he may aspire to the higher and nobler love awakened in his breast by Elizabeth.

The other pilgrims sang psalms of praise, but he scarcely dared to look to Rome in the distance, saying, "God be merciful to me a sinner." While they refreshed themselves and slept in hospices on the way, he made his bed upon the snow. When they walked over the smooth road, he walked among thorns, and when he came to Italy so that not even the fair scenes of that land should give him joy, he blindfolded his eyes and thus journeyed toward the Eternal City.

At last the morn came upon which he was to see the Holy Father, and hope rose in his heart. During the entire day he stood patiently while thousands of others passed by, the ecstasies of heaven on their countenances, and received there the pardon they craved, going away with lighter hearts, gladdened and ready to make a new start.

At last came his turn. He stood in that august presence and waited patiently for the Holy Father's message, waiting and hoping for a kind word to send him on his way rejoicing. Instead there came the thundered words, "If you have associated with demons, then there is no forgiveness for you, neither in heaven nor on Earth. Sooner will this dry staff which I hold in my hand blossom, than that thy sins will be forgiven."

At this heartless announcement the last spark of hope died within Tannhauser, and lust, a thing of blood, lifted its head. His love was turned to hate, and blazing with anger he cursed everything in heaven and on Earth, swearing that if he could not have true love, then he would return to the cave and seek Venus anew, and telling his fellow pilgrims to keep back, he leaves then and journeys back to his native home alone.

Meanwhile the prayers of Elizabeth, the pure and chaste virgin to whom Tannhauser's love had gone out, unceasingly called for forgiveness for the sinner. Hopefully she awaited the return of the pilgrims, but when at last they arrived and Tannhauser was not among them, despair seized her, and feeling that there was no other way she passed out of this phase of life, to present personally her petition at the Throne of Grace before our Heavenly Father. The funeral procession is met by the returning Tannhauser, who is bowed with unspeakable grief at this sight.

Then another band of returning pilgrims arrive, telling of a great miracle which has taken place at Rome. The staff of the Pope had budded to signify that a sinner refused remission on Earth, had found **pardon in heaven.**

Though the legend is clothed in medieval and Catholic phraseology, and though we may discount the idea that any one man has power to forgive sin or deny remission, it contains spiritual truths which are becoming more pertinent with each passing year. It deals with the unpardonable sin: the only sin that cannot be forgiven, but must be expiated. As you know, Jehovah is the highest Initiate of the Moon Period, the ruler of the Angels, who during this present Day of Manifestation work with our humanity through the Moon. He is the author of generation and the prime factor in gestation, the giver of offspring to man and to beast, using the lunar ray as his vehicle of work during the times which are propitious to generation. Jehovah is a jealous God, jealous of his prerogative, and, therefore, when man ate of the tree of knowledge and took the matter of generation into his own hands, he expelled him from paradise to wander in the wilderness of the world. There was no forgiveness. He must expiate it in travail and in pain, reaping the fruit of his transgression.

Before the Fall, humanity had not known either good or evil. They had done what they were told, and nothing else. By taking matters into their own hands, and by the pain and the sorrow which followed their transgression, they learned the difference between good and evil: they became capable of choice. They acquired prerogative. This is the great privilege which more than compensates for the suffering and the sorrow man has endured in expiation of that offense against the Law of Life, which lies in performing the creative act when the stellar rays are unpropitious, thus causing painful parturition, and a multitude of other diseases to which humanity is heir today.

In this connection I may mention that the Moon is the ruler of the sign Cancer, and that cancer, in its malignant form, admits of no cure, no matter how many remedies science may bring forward from time to time. Investigation of the lives of persons who suffer from this disease has proved in every case that the one involved has been sensual in the extreme during previous lives, though I am not prepared to say that this is a law, since a sufficient number of investigations have not been made to establish it. It is, nevertheless, significant that Jehovah, the Holy Spirit, rules generative functions through the Moon, that the Moon governs Cancer, and that those who abuse the sex function in a very marked and bestial degree are later afflicted with the disease called cancer: that that is incurable and thus bears out the saying in the Bible that all things may be forgiven save the sin against the Holy Spirit.

There is a mystic connection between the Cherubim with the flaming sword at the Garden of Eden and the Cherubim with the open flower on the door of Solomon's Temple: between the spear and the Grail cup: between Aaron's rod that budded and the staff of the Pope which flowered and the death of the chaste and pure Elizabeth, by whose intercession the stain was removed from the soul of the erring Tannhauser.

Neither can one who has never known the awful torment of temptation realize the position of one who has fallen. Christ, Himself, felt in the body of Jesus all the passion and all the temptations to which we ourselves are subject, and it is stated that that was for the purpose of making Him merciful unto us as a High Priest. That He was tempted, proves that temptation is in itself not sin. *It is the yielding that is sin;* therefore, He was without sin. Whoever can thus be tempted and withstand, is of course highly evolved; but let us remember that none of the present humanity has yet arrived at that stage of perfection and that we are better men and women for having sinned, and suffered in consequence, until we have become awake to the important fact that the way of the transgressor is hard, and have turned into the pathway of virtue, whereon alone is found inward peace. Such men and women are on a much higher stage of spiritual development than those who have lived lives of purity because of a sheltered environment. This Christ emphasized when He said that there shall be more rejoicing over one sinner who repents than over the ninety-and-nine who need no repentance.

There is a very important distinction between innocence and virtue, and what is more important still, is that *we should realize the fallacy of the double standard of conduct* which gives liberties to or rather condones them in a man, while insisting that one misstep will ruin a woman for life. Were I to choose a wife today, and later learn that her life had been clouded by a mistake for which she had suffered, I should know that such a one had learned to know sorrow, and had engendered compassion and forbearance thereby, and had thus acquired qualities which would make her a better and more sympathetic companion than one who stood "innocent" upon the threshold of life, liable to fall a prey to the first temptation that befell her.

Chapter XVIII

THE ROD THAT BUDDED

IN the prologue of Faust, God is represented as saying, concerning the hero:

"With vision imperfect he serves me now,
But soon I'll lead him where more light appears;
When buds the sapling doth the gardener know,
That flow'r and fruit will grace its coming years."

This is the actual fact concerning all mankind. At the present time we all serve God imperfectly because of our limited vision. We have not the real, true perception of what is wanted and of how we should use the talents wherewith we are now endowed. Nevertheless God, through the process of evolution is constantly leading us into greater and greater light, and by degrees we shall cease to be spiritually barren: We shall flower and bear fruit. Thus we shall be able to serve God as we would and not as we do.

While the foregoing applies to all in general, it applies particularly to those who stand in the limelight as teachers; for naturally, where the light is the strongest, the shadows are also the deepest, and the imperfections of those among us, who must take up the burden of teaching, are naturally more marked on that account.

In the story of Tannhauser, the Pope shuts the door of hope in the face of the penitent because the letter of the law requires it, but not thus is God's mercy frustrated. The Pope's staff blooms to prove that the penitent has been forgiven because of the sincere penitence whereby the evil has been washed from the record made upon the seed atom. Thus by a higher law the lower has been superseded.

There is in this legend of the Pope's staff, a similarity to the tale of the Holy Grail and the spear; to the story of Aaron's rod which also bloomed, and to the staff of Moses that brought the water of life forth from the rock. All have an important bearing upon the problem of the spiritual life of the Disciple who aims to follow the path to the higher life and seeks, like Kundry, to undo the deeds of ill of former lives by a present life of service to the higher self. The legend of the Grail distinguishes between the Grail cup itself and the Cleansing Blood which it held.

The story is told of how Lucifer, when he strove with the Archangel Michael over the body of Moses, lost the choicest gem in his crown. It was dislodged in the struggle. This beautiful gem, comparable to none, was an emerald named "Exilir." It was thrown into the abyss but was recovered by the Angels and from that the chalice or Holy Grail was made which later was used to hold the Cleansing Blood that flowed

The Rod That Budded

from the Savior's side when it had been pierced by the centurion's spear. Let us first note the fact that this jewel was an emerald: it was green, and green is a combination of blue and yellow, and is, therefore, the complementary color of the third primary color, red. In the Physical World red has the tendency to excite and energize, whereas green has a cooling and a soothing effect, but the opposite is true when we look at the matter from the viewpoint of the Desire World. There the complementary color is active, and has the effect upon our desires and emotions which we ascribe to the physical color. Thus the green color of the gem lost by Lucifer shows the nature and effect thereof. This stone is the antithesis of the Philosopher's Stone. It has the power to attract passion and generate love of sex for sex, which is the vice opposite to the chaste and pure love, symbolized by the apocalyptic white stone, which latter is the love of soul for soul. As this effect of the complementary colors is well known, though not consciously realized, we also speak of jealousy, which is engendered by impure love, as the green eyed monster.

The Holy Grail finds its replica in the chalice or seed pod of the plant, which is green. The creative fire slumbers within the seed pod. Likewise the same phenomenon must become manifest within each one who enters upon the quest of the Holy Grail. Will is the male quality of the soul; imagination is the female. When will is the strongest attribute, the soul wears male attire in a certain life, and in another, where the quality of imagination is greater, the female garb is taken. Thus under the Law of Alternation which prevails during the present age of the rainbow, the soul wears a different garment in alternate lives, but whether the gender is feminine or masculine, the organ of the opposite sex is present in an undeveloped state. Thus man is now, and will be so long as the physical body endures, both male and female.

In the hoary past, when his consciousness was focused in the spiritual world, he was a perfect creative unit with both sex organs equally developed as are many flowers today. He was then capable of generating a new body when the old one was worn out, but he was not at that time aware to the same degree as he is now of the fact that he had a body. Then some who were pioneers—some who saw more clearly than others—told to their compeers the astonishing story that man has a body. They were often met with the same skepticism which is now shown to those who affirm that we have a soul.

Thus the symbolical story of Lucifer losing the green gem is the story of how man ceased to know himself and began to know his wife; of how the Grail was lost, and of how it may only be found through the cleansing of the passion filled physical blood which was originally contained in that green vessel.

At a propitious time of the year, but neither before nor after, the rays emanating from the heavenly orbs pierce the planted seed and waken its latent generative force into activity. Then a new plant springs out of the ground to again beautify the Earth. Thus the act of generation is accomplished in perfect harmony with the Law of Nature, and a thing of beauty is generated to adorn the Earth. The result is different in humans since the feminine quality of imagination was roused by Lucifer.

Now the generative act is performed regardless of the propitious solar rays, and as a result sin and death entered the world. From that time the spiritual light has waned, and we are now blind to heaven's glory.

In the hands of the divine leaders of mankind, one of them signified by Aaron, the living rod was a vehicle of power. Later the blooming rod dried up and was laid away in the Ark, but we are not to conclude that there is no redemption on that account, for as man was exiled from the heavenly state when the green gem of passion and desire rolled from the crown of Lucifer, who then led mankind through *generation to degeneration;* so also there is the white stone, the Philosopher's Stone, the symbol of emancipation. By using the power of generation for regeneration, we overcome death and sin. It then endows us with immortality and leads us to Christ.

That is the message of the story of Tannhauser. Passion is poison. Abuse of generation under the sway of Lucifer, has been the means of leading us downward into the gloom of degeneration, but the same power turned into the opposite direction and used for purposes of regeneration is capable of lifting us out of the gloom and elevating us to a heavenly state, when we have thus won the battle. Through passion the Spirit has been crystallized into a body and only by chastity can the fetters be loosed, for *heaven is the home of the virgin* and only in so far as we elevate love from that of sex for sex to the standard of soul for soul can we shatter the shackles that bind us. Then, when we learn to make conception immaculate, saviors will be born who will loose the fetters of sin and sorrow that now bind us.

In carrying out this ideal let us remember, however, that suppression of the sexual desire is not celibacy; the mind must concur and we must willingly abstain from impurity. This can only be done by what the mystic calls *"finding the woman within himself."* (Of course for woman, it is to find the man within herself.) When we have found that, we arrive at the point where we can live the same pure life as the flower.

In this connection it may also be very illuminating to remember that the "Dweller on the Threshold" which we must confront before we can enter the superphysical worlds always has the appearance of a creature of the opposite sex. Yet it seems to be ourselves. It should also be understood that the more licentious or lustful we have been, the worse will be the appearance of this monster, and Parsifal standing before Kundry, when his refusal of compliance has turned her into a virago, is in fact at the very point where the candidate finds himself face to face with the dweller, before the spear is given into his hands.

Lohengrin

The Knight of the Swan

Lohengrin

Chapter XIX

THE KNIGHT OF THE SWAN

AMONG the operas of Wagner there is, perhaps, none which is so universally enjoyed by the large majority of people who see it, as Lohengrin. This is probably because the story seems, on cursory examination, to be very simple and beautiful. The music is of an unusually exquisite character, which appeals to all in a manner which is not equalled by the author's other operas founded upon myths such as Parsifal, the Ring of the Niebelung, or even Tannhauser.

Although these last named productions affect people who hear them powerfully for their spiritual good(whether they are aware of the fact or not), it is nevertheless, a fact that they are not enjoyed by the majority, particularly in America, where the spirit of mysticism is not so strong as it is in Europe.

It is different with Lohengrin. Here there is a story of the time when knighthood was in flower, and although there is an embellishment of magic in the advent of Lohengrin and the swan in response to the prayer of Elsa, this is only as a pretty poetical fancy without deeper meaning. In this myth is revealed one of the supreme requirements of Initiation—faith.

Whoever has not this virtue will never attain; its possession covers a multitude of shortcomings in other directions.

The plot is briefly as follows: The heir of the Duchy of Brabant has disappeared. He is but a child, and the brother of Elsa, the heroine of the play, who is accused in the opening scene by Ortrud and Telramund, her enemies, of having done away with this young brother in order that she may obtain possession of the principality. In consequence she has been summoned before the royal court to defend herself against her accusers, but at the opening scene no knight as yet has appeared to espouse her cause and slay her traducers. Then there appears on the river a swan, upon which stands a knight, who comes up to the place where court is being held. He jumps ashore and offers to defend Elsa on condition that she marry him. To this she readily agrees, for he is no stranger; she has often seen him in her dreams and learned to love him. In the duel between the unknown knight and Telramund, the latter is thrown, but his life is magnanimously spared by the conqueror, who then claims Elsa as his bride. He had, however, made another condition; namely, that she may never ask him who he is and whence he came. As he appears so good and so noble, and as he has come in answer to her prayer, she makes no objection to this condition either, and the couple retire to the bridal chamber.

Although temporarily defeated, Ortrud and Telramund do not by any means give up their conspiracy against Elsa, and their next move is to poison her mind against her noble protector, so that she may send him away and then be again at their mercy; for they hope, eventually, themselves to secure the principality to which Elsa and her brother are the rightful heirs. With this end in view both present themselves at Elsa's door and succeed in getting a hearing. They profess to be exceedingly penitent for what they have done, and very solicitous for the welfare of Elsa. It pains them very much, they say, that she has been taken in by someone whose name she does not even know, and who is so afraid that his identity be known that he has forbidden her, on pain of his leaving her to ask him his name.

There must be something in his life of which he is ashamed, they argue, which will not bear the light of day, else why should he wish to deny the one to whom he is willing to link his whole life, knowledge of his identity and antecedents?

By means of these arguments they arouse a doubt in Elsa's soul, and after some conversation she goes in to Lohengrin, changed. He notices the difference in her, and asks the cause. Finally she admits that she feels uncertain about him and that she would like to know his name. Thereby she has broken the condition which he has imposed upon her, and he tells her that now, having expressed a doubt in him, it will be impossible for him to remain. Neither tears nor protestations can change this resolve, so they go together to the river where Lohengrin calls his trusty swan, and when that appears he reveals his identity, saying, "I am Lohengrin, the son of Parsifal." The swan which then comes, is changed and stands before them all as the brother of Elsa. He then becomes her protector in place of the departing Lohengrin.

As said, the story of Lohengrin contains one of the most important lessons to be learned on the path of attainment. No one will ever attain Initiation till that has been learned. In order that we may properly grasp this point, let us first look at the symbol of the swan and see what is behind it and why the symbol is used. Those who have seen the opera, Parsifal, or who have read attentively the literature on the Grail, are already acquainted with the fact that swans were the emblems worn by all the Knights of the Grail.

In the opera, itself, two swans are mentioned as preparing a healing bath for the suffering King Amfortas. Parsifal is represented as shooting one of these swans,

THE KNIGHT OF THE SWAN

and a great deal of sorrow is manifested by the Knights of the Grail at this unwarranted cruelty.

The swan is capable of moving in several elements. It may fly in the air with great swiftness; it also propels itself majestically upon the water; and by means of its long neck it may even explore the depths and investigate whatever may be found upon the bottom of a not too deep pond. It is, therefore, an apt symbol of the Initiate, who, on account of the power developed within him, is capable of elevating himself to higher realms, and moving in different worlds. As the swan flies through space, so may one who has developed the powers of his soul body travel in that over mountains and lakes; as the swan dives below the surface of the water, so may also the Initiate go underneath the surface of the deep in his soul body, which is not in danger from fire, earth, air, or water. In fact, that is one of the first things that the Invisible Helpers have to be taught: that they are immune from any danger which may befall them in the physical body, when they are invested with the Golden Wedding Garment of which we have spoken so much. Thus they may enter a burning building with immunity, there assisting those who are in danger, sometimes in a most miraculous manner; or they may be on board a sinking ship giving encouragement to those who are about to face the great change.

The ancient Norse mythology tells us how noble warriors of old, when they had fought the battle and had finally been overcome or mortally wounded, sang their swan song. But let it not be supposed for a moment that it was only the brutal fight fought upon the battle field with sword and lance that was meant; rather it was the inner fight, the hidden meaning, that a noble soul who had fought the battle of life well, at the last when he had attained to that which was possible in those days, sang his swan song: that is he took his oath of Initiation and became capable of entering another realm to help others there as he had helped them here; for it was ever the sacred duty of a noble knight to succor those who were weak and heavy laden.

Elsa is the daughter of a king. She is thus of the highest and most noble birth. No one who is not thus *well born* can lay claim to the services of such a knight as Lohengrin in that manner; that is to say of course, there is in humanity neither high nor low, save as we stand in the scale of evolution. When a soul has been long upon the stage of life, has gone to school for many, many lives, then gradually it acquires that nobility which comes from learning the lessons and working along the lines laid down by the schoolmasters, our Elder Brothers, who are now teaching us the lessons of life. The nobility earned by eagerness to do deeds of mercy for our less highly advanced fellow beings, is the key to their favor, and therefore when Elsa was in distress, a noble soul is sent to teach and guide her.

In the Book of Revelation we read about the mystic

marriage of the Bride and the Lamb. There is that marriage in every soul's experience, and always under similar circumstances. One of the first requisites is that the soul must have been forsaken by every one else: it must stand alone without a single friend in the world. When that point has been attained, when the soul sees no succor from any earthly source, when it turns with its whole heart to heaven and prays for deliverance, then comes the deliverer and also the offer of marriage. In other words, the true Teacher always comes in response to the earnest prayers of the aspirant, but not till he has forsaken the world and been forsaken by it. He offers to take care of one who is thus anxious for guidance, and forthwith conquers untruth with the sword of truth, but having given this proof, henceforth he requires an absolute unquestioning faith. *Please remember*—let it imprint itself upon your mind, let it sear itself into your very being with letters of fire, that having come in answer to the prayer, (which is not only words but a life of aspiration) the indubitable, unquestionable proof is given of the power and ability of the Teacher to teach, to guide, and to help; and then the requirement is made that henceforth there must be absolute faith in him, otherwise it becomes impossible for him to work with the aspirant.

That is the great lesson that is taught by Lohengrin, and it is of supreme importance, for there are thousands upon thousands walking the streets in many cities today, looking hither and thither, seeking a Teacher. Some pretend to have found him, or have deceived themselves into that belief; but the requirement that is enunciated in Lohengrin is an actual requirement. The Teacher must, will, and does prove his ability. He is known by his fruits; then in return he demands *loyalty,* and unless this faith, this loyalty, this readiness to serve, this willingness to do whatever is required, is forthcoming from the aspirant, the relationship will be terminated. No matter how hot may be the tears of repentance which might follow in the case of the aspirant who had failed in his loyalty to the Teacher, no matter how sincere his repentance; the next opportunity will not be forthcoming in the present life.

Therefore, it is of the very greatest importance that those who are seeking Initiation should understand that there is something due them from the professed teacher, before they accept him. He must show the fruits of his work, for as Christ said, "By their fruits ye shall know them." This the genuine Teacher always does without being asked, *and without seeming to do so* or to want to give a sign. He always furnishes some evidence to which the mind of the aspirant can cling as an indubitable proof of his superior knowledge and ability. When that has then been demonstrated, *it is absolutely essential that loyalty to the Teacher must follow;* and no matter who says this, that, or the other thing, the aspirant should not be disturbed, but cling steadfastly to the proven fact, stick to that which he believes to be true and faithfully uphold the one to whom he looks for teaching; for unless that faith is there, there is no use in continuing the relationship.

It is very significant, however, that Elsa's brother was, as we learn from the final scene, the swan which had carried Lohengrin to his sister, and who was changed back to his natural shape when Lohengrin departed. He had been through Initiation. He, no doubt, knew of his sister's plight, as one soul who is advanced and studying along these lines knows of another's struggles, but although he saw the predicament of this fair aspirant, or sister soul, he had no fear, for was he not the means of bringing to her the succor that she might have had permanently had she been as faithful as he?

The End.

Index

	Page
Aaron, rod of, power of religion	81
vehicle of power	158
Alberich, symbolizes pioneers of mankind	76
Alternation of sexes in Aryan Epoch	152
America, electric atmosphere	130
spirit of mysticism lacking in	158
Angels, led by Jehovah	36
negative influence of	27
Apes, degeneration of	36
under care of Lucifer Spirits	36
Apocalypse and Twilight of the Gods	119
Apples, golden, life-giving food of gods	79
Archetypes, copies of, perishable	46
Ark, lungs symbolized by	124
Arts, three	50
Aryana, atmospheric conditions of	132
world of today	77
Aspirant, desertion of	163
must cultivate self-reliance	23
transmutes passion in blood	32
Atlantean Epoch, savagery of	118
Atlanteans, childlike nature of	75
lacked individualized Ego	75
inner perception of	75
symbolized by Rhine maidens	74
Atlantis, childlike people of	75
dense foggy atmosphere of	74
Atmosphere, clearing of, aids perception of selfhood	77
Attainment by arduous struggle	22
Attraction, Law of	29
Bifrost, rainbow bridge	79
Bird, symbolizes quickening spirit	59
Black magic, symbols of	25
Black magician, enters and leaves body by feet	25
vampires on sex force of others	32

INDEX

	Page
Blood, built by Spirit	31
cleansed, regenerative power of	32
extract of vital body	31
individual structure of	31
iron in, due to Mars	31
seat of soul	30
Brunhilde, favorite daughter of Wotan	85
sleep of	93
spirit of truth	85
Cain, Sons of, descendants of Lucifer Spirits	35
drawn into statecraft	43
Cancer, disease of, result of past immorality	146
Causation, cancellation of duties of	89
Chivalry in Aryan Epoch	119
Christ, aid of, to fallen	41
evolution of principles of, work of Western World	71
every Son of Seth to leave all for	42
will return in vital body	24
Christ, see also Earth Spirit.	
Christ Jesus, our High Priest	147
temptation of	147
Church's creeds, do not satisfy	97
deprive man of individuality	95
Circle dance, of marching orbs	9
Civilization, follows Sun's path	73
Cleansing Blood of Grail	150
Color, function of	50
Compassion, known through experience	34
Compensation, given for bodily action	37
Courage, necessary in development of soul	138
Creed, causes decay of religion	81
purpose of	83
Crystallization, caused by passion	36
Curiosity, danger of	114
Dead, lamentations for, cause grief to	111
Desire body, emotions of easily dissipated	72
less retentive than vital body	72
Desire World, complementary colors active in	151
illusions of	101
realm of color	52
Disciple, seeks to undo evil of past lives	150
Discord, contrasting value of	132

168   MYSTERIES OF THE GREAT OPERAS

	Page
Dogma, usefulness of	83
Double standard, fallacy of	147
Dweller on Threshold	154
Earth, activity below outer stratum	19
coming change of	124
nine strata of	19
past connection of with planets	30
Earth lives, test of knowledge in	116
Earth Spirit, controls Earth from within	25
liberation of	20
living reality of, revealed in Initiation	19
power in name of	18
East, etheric atmosphere of	73
Eden, Garden of	74
Effort, advancement gained through	82
Ego, bisexual state of	141
directs action by thought	52
enveloped in ring of vehicles	80
symbolized by Ring	98
Egotism, supplanted brotherhood	36
Emotion, intense, necessity for	38
Eternal Feminine, creative force in universe	46
Europe, mystic atmosphere of	130
Evolution, unceasing effort in	82
Exilir, antithesis of Philosopher's Stone	151
color of soothing effect	151
Grail made from	150
Experience, post-mortem, record of	113
Fafner, giant builder of limitation	80
spirit of desire	98
Faith, in Christ, redemptive power of	42
in Teacher, necessity for	164
Fasolt, giant builder of limitation	80
Fates, three, *see Norns*	
Father, the macrocosm	28
Father, religion of	20
Faust, evolved humanity	11
Son of Cain	42
story of, is a myth	6
symbolical of the seeking soul	24, 27
tells story of the World Temple	46
Fenris, the atmosphere	121
Fire, of Aryan Age	120

	Page
Forgiveness of sin	150
Form, function of	50
Freemasonry	6
Freya, Norse counterpart of Venus	79
Friday, dedicated to Venus	79
Frost Giants, existence of, before Earth	90
nature forces	90
Gamuret, the man of the world	60
Garment of the Ego, the soul	52
Generation, relation of, to solar ray	152
Giants, builders of limitation	80
Gimle, New Earth	122
God, life of, invests every atom of matter	15
perpetual development of	10
Gods, constant evolution	77
limit themselves by ring	77
remain until end of epoch	80
warders of religions	80
Goethe, enlightened Initiate	6
Grail, Castle of	32
Cleansing Blood contained in	150
found only by conquest of passion	152
quest for, causes spiritual strife	22
Grane, steed of discernment	106
Group Spirit, influences animals by mental pictures	72
work through animals' desire bodies	72
Gutrune, honors of the world	119
Heaven, ideals attained	46
Region of Concrete Thought	104
Heavens, harmony of, changes every moment	8, 9
Hel, ruler of the indolent	88
symbolical of death	121
Herod, Castle of and Castle of Grail	32
Herzleide, sorrow	60
Hierarchies, Creative, constant evolution of	90
Higher knowledge, follows mastery of lower	16
Higher law, supersedes lower	150
Higher nature, struggle with lower	22
Hoard of Niebelung, material acquisitions of	118
Hunding, spirit of convention	91
Hypnotic power, helmet of illusion	117
Ideals, etched into higher vehicles	6

	Page
Imagination, aroused by Lucifer	153
female quality of Spirit	153
Immaculate conception	154
Inactivity, power of, to shorten life	29
Incubi, evil obsessing entities	130
Initiate, master of different elements	161
Initiation, opened up by Christ	61
reveals Earth Spirit	19
unveils mystery of Earth's constitution	20
words of power given in	18
Inner life, completeness of	51
emotional and mental	52
Iron, is a Mars metal	30
Jealousy engendered by Exilir	151
Jehovah, author of generation	146
guided mankind from without	25
highest Initiate of Moon Period	145
ruler of Angels	36
Jesus, vital body of, Christ's vehicle at future coming	20
Christ entered Earth by means of	25
preserved at centre of Earth	20
Job, vanguard of race	7, 9, 11
Jupiter, Thor, Norse counterpart of	79
Keynote, each star has own	8
Killing, by proxy	59
Klingsor	55
Knight, he who travels path of attainment	138
Knighthood, duties of	138
Knowledge, growth of, related to vital body	31
interior state of	31
responsibility, increases with	115
Knowledge, higher, only follows mastery of worldly information	16
Knowledge, tree of	145
Kundry, the body	67
the Dweller of Parsifal	154
the lower nature	66
Liberation, freedom from rebirth	67
Life Spirit, the Christ principle in man	71
extracts as pabulum intellectual soul	71
Life, tree of, *see* Yggdrasil.	
Light waves, transmuted to sound	8

INDEX

	Page
Loge, guardian of flame	88
related to Saturn	79
spirit of deceit	79
Love, elevation of standards of	129
Lower nature, affected by myths	7
plotting of	97
Lucifer, arouses imagination	153
beneficent influence of	9
green gem of	152
imbued man with ambition	76
Mars Spirit	79
spirit of negation	79
was attracted by mental attitude of Faust	24
Lucifer Spirits, evolve by intensity of feeling induced in man	88
fallen Angels	86
from Mars	81
have freed man from angelic domination	35
incite war and bloodshed	39
progenitors of Sons of Cain	85
selfish influence of	27
stir passions of lower nature	88
Lucifer Spirits, ultimately produce good through suffering	39
Luck, result of merit	37
Lunar ray, vehicle of gestation	145
Lungs, symbolized by Ark	124
Man in past, hermaphrodite	152
led by Angels	27
led by Lucifer Spirits	27
past consciousness of	152
Marguerite, the sinning soul	41
ward of Sons of Seth	35
Matter, God's life invests	15
Mediums, control of, by evil entities	130
Mercury, Norse counterpart of Wotan	78
Michael, Archangel, Lucifer struggles with	150
Midgaard Serpent, the ocean	88
Mime, the lower nature	97
symbolizes dense body	99
well of, bestows knowledge of the past	90
Minstrels, educators of Middle Ages	128
influence of, on public opinion	128
were Initiates	139

	Page
Mistakes, educational value of	13
Mountain of Venus	130
Music, language of Thought World	52
pleases, interspersed with dissonance	9
Myths, effects of, on man's evolution	73
given by great teachers	6
ideals ingrained by	6
seven interpretations of	59
veiled spiritual truths	72
Name, is a sound	18
Nature, feminine creative force	46
Nature forces, see Frost Giants.	
New race, to be offshoot of American	124
Nidhog, spirit of envy	88
Niebelung, children of Wotan	85
Noah, kindled first fire	120
Norns, controlled by law	89
the Three Fates	89
Nostradamus, mentioned	15
Nothung, courage of despair	87
Ocean to pass away	122
Odin, see Wotan	
Orlog, destiny	90
Panorama of Life, see Life panorama.	
Paracelsus, on obsessing entities	130
Parsifal, spear of	81
Parsifal, symbolizes Spirit	26, 27, 67
Passion, aroused by Lucifer Spirits	35
awakened man's individuality	35
causes sickness	35
crystallizing power of	36
Past lives, forgetfulness of	112
pride of	114
Pentagram, symbolism	24, 25
Philosopher's Stone, chaste love symbolized by	151
symbol of redemption	153
Physical World, realm of form	52
Pioneers, need of	83
Pituitary body, development of soul power in	24
Planets, movements of	74
Earth's close connection with	30
Power, occult, to be used unselfishly	97
Priestcraft, Sons of Seth	43

	Page
Progress, necessity for slow	16
penalty in laws of	134
Pythagoras, mentioned song of the spheres	8
Rainbow, first seen in Aryana	79
remains till end of era	80
significance of	120
Rainbow bridge, Bifrost	79
reflection of heavenly fire	120
Rebirth, alternation of sex during	129
taught in Scandinavian mythology	109
Recording Angels, infallibility of	82
Reincarnation, *see* Rebirth.	
Religion, decay of due to creed	81
destroyed by political affiliations	81
forswore love	84
frees from illusion	78
perfect, impossible to present humanity	80
relation of, to love	84
shows way to truth and life	78
symbols of	81
Religions, all imbued with spirit of love	91
various, form steps in man's evolution	80
Renunciation of the world, inevitable	60
Repetition, keynote of vital body	71
Retina, of eye, may be shattered by direct light of Sun	16
Rhinegold, Ring of, dogma and creed	82
Universal Spirit	76
Right, criterion of, determined by evolution	118
Righteousness, future universality of	43
Ring, symbol of limitation	77
symbol of Spirit's immortality	78
symbolizes Ego	78
Rose Cross, Brothers of, foster self-reliance	23
Sacrifice, Law of, greater than Law of Self-preservation	98
Salvation, intended for all	83
Second Advent	25
Second sight, past prevalence of	111
Seed pod of plant and Holy Grail	152
Selfhood, protecting power of	37
Self-reliance, necessary for aspirant	23
Seth, Sons of, negative character	40
the priestcraft	35
Sex, pertains to dense vehicle only	152

	Page
Sex force, extract of vital body	31
transmuted in pituitary body	24
Sexes, alternation of	141
equality of	129
Sickness, attendant upon soul growth	138
Siegfried, represents higher self	96
seeker of truth	86
Sieglinda, enslaved by public opinion	87
Sin, unpardonable	146
Skuld, one of the Fates	89
Snake, symbolical of rebirth	55
Solomon, an incarnation of Jesus	42
Son of Seth	42
Sorrow, educational effects of	148
Soul, freedom in choice of	12
Soul body, development of	161
Soul growth, slow inner process of	32
through good deeds	23
Sound, power of	18
Spear, power of religion	81
spiritual power used unselfishly	66
Spheres, song of	9
Spirit, bi-sexual state of	152
entrance or exit from same door	21
integral part of God	13
primarily innocent	13
ring of, causes limitation	77
Spirits of elements	130
Spirit world, lies about us	15
Spiritual realms, earthly elements nonexistent in	121
Stars, circle dance of	9
discord of, develops individuality	9
have individualized keynote	8
Stellar influences on propagation	146
Succubi, evil possessing entities	130
Suffering, God gives aid to	41
purifying power of	39
Swan, emblem of Grail Knights	160
symbol of Initiate	161
Swan Song, vow of Initiation	162
Tannhauser, man's Spirit at one stage of evolution	129
Tarncap, helmet of illusion	117

INDEX

	Page
Teacher, comes in answer to prayer	163
enabled only to point the way	23
fidelity to	164
known by his fruits	164
Teachers, spiritual, uplift mankind	6, 53
Temple builder, man is	29
Temptation, necessity of	13, 62
persistence of	41
sin in yielding to	147
strengthening of moral nature in	12
Thor, Norse counterpart of Jupiter	79
Thought, attractive power of	130
realm of tone	52
Thought, World of, home of Ego	52
Tone, beauty of induces spiritual good	157
function of	50
Tree of knowledge	145
Tree of life, *see* Yggdrasil.	
Truth, achieved by conquest over limitation	92
the bride of its discoverer	106
contends upon side of truth seeker	91
exists in Region of Concrete Thought	101
knows no boundaries	80
means to an end	101
must be brought down to physical realm	101
must be divorced from earthly ambition	98
world's antagonism to	102
Universal Spirit, the Rhinegold	74
Unpardonable sin	145
Unselfishness, necessity for	65
Urd, fountain of, renews life	89
spins our past destiny	89
Valhal, limitations of	82
the Ring of Creed	91
Valkuerie, symbolical of virtue	85
Valplads, battle field of truth	85
Venus, Freya, Norse counterpart of	79
Venus, Mountain of	130
Venus of Tannhauser, etheric entity	130
Verdande, breaks thread of our future	89
Virtue, developed by suffering	13
distinguished from innocence	63

	Page
Vital body, capable of levitation	25
extracts of	31
repetition, keynote of	71
retentiveness of	72
seen at death	111
vehicle of Christ at Second Coming	25
Walsungs, children of Wotan	85
pioneers demanding free will	84
War, incited by Lucifer Spirits	39
Water, deities of	79
Water of life, spiritual impetus	90
Wedding Garment, construction of	124
etheric vehicle necessary for new race	124
Wednesday, dedicated to Mercury	78
West, etheric atmosphere of, conduces to spiritual perception	73
White Stone, the Philosopher's Stone	151
Will, male quality of Spirit	151
Wisdom, acquired only by well-doing	37
Witches' kitchen, each must enter	37
Wolfram, exponent of spiritual love	137
humanity becomes	139
Woman, equality of	128
place of	129
Word of power	18
World Temple, two classes of humanity build	46
Wordly possessions, desire for	98
Wotan, chief of Hierarchies	90
claims only the brave who die for truth	82
God of the age of air	122
God of wisdom	90
spear of, the power of creed	91
Teutonic counterpart of Mercury	78
warder of creeds	99
Yggdrasil, lives by love	88
tree of life and being	88

The Rosicrucian Cosmo-Conception

Was received from the Brothers of the Rose Cross and published to the world

By Max Heindel

Revealing a New Phase of the Christian Religion

FOR THE NEW AGE NOW AT HAND

Giving the Occult Knowledge whereby the inquiring Mind may find Christ when it is unable to find Him by Faith Alone.

IT INCLUDES:

The Evolutionary Mission of Christ.

A description of the Superphysical Worlds to which we proceed after death.

The Facts about Rebirth.

The Sixth Sense and How to Obtain Firsthand information regarding the Spiritual Planes.

• • •

This Epoch Marking Work Gives the Solution to the World's Present Great Unrest.

• • •

Exhaustive Topical and Alphabetical Indexes

702 Pages.   Cloth Bound.

• • •

THE ROSICRUCIAN FELLOWSHIP

Mt. Ecclesia
Oceanside, California, U.S.A.